SHARPEN YOUR TEAM'S SKILLS IN

*E*FFECTIVE

SELLING

Other titles in this series

Sharpen your skills in motivating people to perform
Trevor Bentley 007 709072 1

Sharpen your team's skills in developing strategy
Susan Clayton 007 709281 3

Sharpen your team's skills in supervision
Susan Clayton 007 709280 5

Sharpen your team's skills in creativity
Trevor Bentley 007 709282 1

Sharpen your team's skills in coaching
Tony Voss 007 709278 3

Sharpen your team's skills in project management
Jean Harris 007 709140 X

Sharpen your team's skills in people skills
Di Kamp 007 709276 7

Sharpen your team's skills in time management
Jane Allan 007 709275 9

SHARPEN YOUR TEAM'S SKILLS IN

*E*FFECTIVE

SELLING

Trevor Bentley

The McGraw-Hill Companies

London · New York · St Louis · San Francisco · Auckland · Bogotá · Caracas
Lisbon · Madrid · Mexico · Milan · Montreal · New Delhi · Panama · Paris
San Juan · São Paulo · Singapore · Sydney · Tokyo · Toronto

Published by

McGraw-Hill Publishing Company

Shoppenhangers Road, Maidenhead, Berkshire SL6 2QL, England
Telephone: 01628 23432
Fax: 01628 770224

British Library Cataloguing in Publication Data
Bentley, Trevor J.
   Sharpen your team's skills in effective selling.—
   1. Employees—Training of   2. Selling
   I. Title   II. Effective selling
   658.8'5
   ISBN 0 07 709279 1

Library of Congress Cataloging-in-Publication Data
Bentley, Trevor J.
   Sharpen your team's skills in effective selling / Trevor Bentley.
      p.   cm.
   Based on: The ASTD trainer's sourcebook. Sales / Herbert R. Miller.
   New York: McGraw-Hill, c 1995.
      ISBN 0-07-709279-1
      1. Sales personnel—Training of.   2. Selling—Problems, exercises,
   etc.   I. Miller, Herbert R. ASTD trainer's sourcebook. Sales.
   II. Title.
   HF5439.8.B46   1996
   658.3'1245—dc20

Based on an original book by Herbert Miller, *The ASTD Trainer's Sourcebook: Sales Training*, McGraw-Hill, New York, 1995.

McGraw-Hill

A Division of *The McGraw·Hill* Companies

1 2 3 4 CUP 9 9 8 7 6

Typesetting by David Gregson Associates, Beccles, Suffolk
Printed and bound in Great Britain at the University Press, Cambridge

Printed on permanent paper in compliance with ISO Standard 9706

CONTENTS

EXERCISES

Part Five—Completing the Sale

SCENARIOS

SERIES PREFACE

This series of books focuses on sharpening the performance of your team by providing a range of training and support materials. These materials can be used in a variety of ways to improve the knowledge and skills of your team.

Creating high performance is achieved by paying attention to three key elements:

- The skills (competencies) of your people
- The way these skills are applied
- The support your people receive from you in applying their skills.

SKILL DEVELOPMENT

The books have been designed so that they can be used as individual workbooks

The books in this series will provide materials for the development of a range of skills on a subject-by-subject basis. Each book will provide information and exercises in manageable chunks (lessons), which will be presented in a format which will allow you to choose the most appropriate way to deliver them to your staff. The contents will consist of all you need to guide your staff to a full understanding of the subject.

There are at least four ways you could choose to guide the learning of your team; these are:

- Training sessions
- Learning groups
- Open learning
- Experiential learning.

TRAINING SESSIONS

These can be run by bringing your people together and guiding them step by step through the materials, including the exercises. During these sessions you can invite your people to interact with you and the materials by asking questions and relating the materials to their current work. The materials will provide you with the detailed information you need to present the subject to your team.

LEARNING GROUPS

This approach means dividing your team into small groups (two, three or four people) and having a brief session with each group introducing them to the materials. Each group then works through the materials and meets with you from time to time to assess progress and receive your guidance.

OPEN LEARNING

This approach invites your people to use the materials at their own speed and in their own way. This is a form of individual learning which can be managed by regular meetings between you and your team as individuals or in a group. The process is started by introducing the materials to your team and agreeing some 'learning outcomes' to be achieved.

EXPERIENTIAL LEARNING

This calls for you to invite your team to examine the materials using the exercises as a focus, and then to get them to relate what they are learning directly to real-life situations in the workplace. This experience of learning is then shared and discussed by the team as a whole.

The books in the series have been designed to enable these four approaches to be used, as well as other ways that you might think are more appropriate to your team's specific needs.

APPLYING SKILLS

Time spent developing skills can be wasted if people do not have the opportunity to practise the skills. It is important that you consider this aspect of performance before embarking on a particular programme. It is useful if you are able to clearly identify opportunities for practising skills and discussing these with your team. Providing opportunities for practising and further developing competency is part and parcel of the whole approach of this series.

PROVIDING SUPPORT

Once people have acquired a new skill and have been provided with opportunities to apply it, they still need your support and coaching while they are experimenting with using the skill. The opening book in this series, *Sharpen your skills in motivating people to perform*, provides clear guidance on how to help people to develop their skills and then how to provide experience, practice and support as they use their skills.

Before starting work with your team on the materials in this book, I suggest you do the following:

- Review the materials yourself
- Plan the approach you are going to follow
- Discuss what you are planning with your team
- Agree some learning outcomes
- Indicate how you are going to support your team during the learning process.

You can also make the materials relate to your specific circumstances by doing three things:

- Add local 'colour'
- Adjust the emphasis
- Integrate your own materials.

The authors in the series have endeavoured to provide a range of materials that is comprehensive and will support you and your team. I hope that during this process you learn from and enjoy the experience.

Dr Trevor J. Bentley
Series Editor

ABOUT THE EDITORIAL PANEL

Susan Clayton is a leading contributor to the use and development of Gestalt philosophy and practice in organizations. Focusing on human processes, she enables managers and their staff to achieve business goals that depend on managing people. Her skill in raising awareness of how people relate to each other can forge supportive alliances and powerful co-operative relationships. Her approach includes helping people to manage blocks and difficulties in their contact with others, clearing the way for work and business relationships to move forward and grow.

Susan works with managers at all levels. Her interventions have aided groups in turmoil, managers needing to reach common agreement and individuals needing mentoring and coaching support. She helps organizations understand how to manage in a way that creates trust, respect and clarity in human relationships.

Mike Taylor is a consultant involved in the design, implementation and facilitation of personal and team development programmes within organizations. After graduating in 1987, he worked with two outdoor management training providers, both as a manager and tutor. His work has a strong focus on the use of experiential learning in developing managers, mainly within larger organizations.

He also works with groups and single individuals in running meetings and events which help teams and individuals explore working practices and approaches. More recently he has developed an interest in Gestalt as a way of understanding group processes. He is a member of the Association for Management Education and Development.

Dr Tony Voss is a counsellor, consultant and trainer. He originally trained as a chemist before working in environmental research developing sea-going computer systems and information technology, and later in the computer industry as a project manager, consultant and quality manager. Tony has a particular interest in enabling people to contribute fully and creatively to their endeavours, and sees this as benefiting individuals, their organizations and society at large. He is an Accredited Counsellor with the British Association for Counselling and has also trained in Gestalt over four years.

Tony works with those wanting to develop their organizations and people, and those dealing with particular challenges in their working life. His clients also include those exploring the role of work in their life, as well as those with more personal issues.

About the Author

Dr Trevor Bentley, series editor for this series, is a freelance organizational consultant, a facilitator and a writer. Prior to becoming a consultant and while working as a senior executive, Trevor carried out a major research project into decision making and organization structures for which he was awarded his PhD. Over the last 20 years he has had a wide range of experience working with organizations in over 20 countries. Trevor has trained for four years with Gestalt South West and attended Gestalt workshops in the UK and Europe. He now applies a Gestalt approach in his work.

Trevor has written 20 books and over 250 articles on business related issues. His background includes careers as a management accountant, financial director, computer systems designer, a management services manager, a human computer interface consultant, a trainer and a business manager. His current area of interest is in the application of a Gestalt approach to solving problems of organizational harmony. This includes culture change, performance management, team facilitation, executive coaching, mentoring and integrated supervision.

CHAPTER 1

Introduction to Effective Selling

KEY LEARNING POINTS

The key learning point in this chapter is:

■ **To gain an overview of the steps to effective selling that are dealt with in this book**

INTRODUCTION

This book is divided into five sections. The first deals with communication skills and the next four deal with the four phases of the selling process. The sections are:

■ Communication skills
■ Earn the right
■ Understand the need
■ Make a recommendation
■ Complete the sale.

We believe that this sales process is as applicable to 'one call-close' situations as it is to more complex 'multi-call' sales cycles.

The basic philosophy underlying this sales process and our approach to it is quite simple:

- A salesperson is there to sell
- Customers are there because they *really* want to and/or need to buy
- Salespeople do *not* have a right granted by a higher-being to pursue the sale—*they must earn it.*

Given this philosophy and the context of our sales process, we focus, in this book, on four important sales skills and five basic communication skills. These are:

- Sales skills
  - Building rapport
  - Qualifying opportunities
  - Describing benefits
  - Handling obstacles
- Communication skills
  - Listening
  - Verifying
  - Observing
  - Questioning
  - Explaining

EFFECTIVE SELLING

Effective selling requires two things from your people:

- A 'way of thinking' about the sales situation that provides motivation and direction for selling—a *mindset*
- A 'way of doing things' during the sales situation that is based on techniques required for success in selling—a *skill set.*

The *mindset* that is appropriate for your particular business situation needs to be considered and defined

The *mindset* that will provide motivation and direction for your people consists of two parts:

- *Key assumptions* about the sales situation, and why salespeople and customers are in a sales situation in the first place

■ *A well-defined sales process* A process that will help structure your people's actions and lead to efficiency from the first meeting with the customer to successful completion of the sale.

Likewise, the *skill set* consists of two parts:

The *skill set* covered in this book should deal with most sales situations, but you might need to check if this is true for your particular situation

■ *Communication skills* Skills that help people to effectively gather information from their customers and present information to their customers throughout the sales process
■ *Sales skills* Skills that tend to be key to success in particular phases of the sales process.

Figure 1.1 depicts the four phases of the sales process, along with the communication skills and four sales skills that are key to effectively using this sales process.

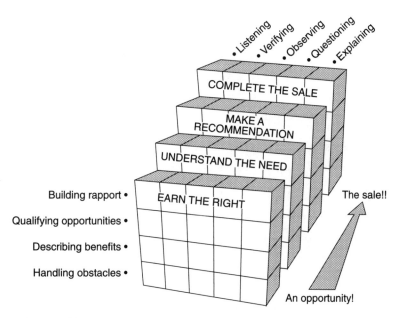

FIGURE 1.1: Effective selling

Source: Miller, H., *The ASTD Trainer's Sourcebook: Sales Training*, McGraw-Hill New York, 1995, p. 387

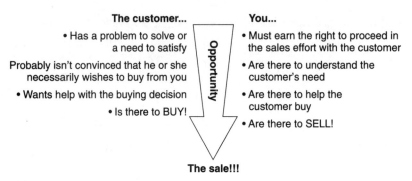

FIGURE 1.2: Key assumptions

Source: Miller, H., *The ASTD Trainer's Sourcebook: Sales Training*, McGraw-Hill New York, 1995, p. 363

KEY ASSUMPTIONS

There are a number of assumptions that are key to success as a salesperson. The first two are critical:

- From the salesperson's point of view, the sale begins as *an opportunity.*
- The challenge is to move from the opportunity to success— *completing the sale.*

Having made these assumptions it is important that your people make the following assumptions about the reasons that they and their customers find themselves together in a sales situation. These assumptions are shown in Figure 1.2. The key message in this figure can be summarized as follows:

- In a sales situation, it is the salesperson's job to *learn about the customer's need* and then to *complete the sale.*

The sales process, along with the application of key communication and sales skills, is designed to facilitate learning about the customer's needs and completing the sale.

Exercise 1—Your sales experiences

This is an exercise to get your staff to highlight their current sales experiences from several viewpoints. Ask them to:

- Think of recent sales experiences you have had—as a customer, a salesperson, and an observer
- Think about the factors that were positive or good about these experiences and those that were unsatisfactory—even unpleasant
- Make brief notes about these factors in the spaces below.

Your experiences as:	The positive, the good	The unsatisfactory
A customer		
A salesperson		
An observer		

THE SALES PROCESS

The sales process that is recommended here is divided into four phases. As you read the definition of each phase it is important to keep the following points in mind. Depending on the nature of the sales situation:

The four phases are:

- Earn the right
- Understand the need
- Make a recommendation
- Complete the sale

- All four phases might be used in one interaction with the customer before completion of the sale
- There may be several sales interactions, or sales calls, as the four phases are worked through and a sale completed.

EARN THE RIGHT

This first phase is key to the success of your people's sales efforts. This is the time when they and their customer meet—a time when they form their first impressions of one another, for better or worse. Hopefully for the better, of course.

An important aspect of this phase is *building rapport*—one of the skills described later in this chapter. A key result of successfully beginning to build rapport is *earning the right to proceed*—hence the name of this phase.

- Salespeople must build the basic level of trust and confidence that encourages their customers to stay with them, and essentially grant them the right to move forward with the sales effort
- Such a level of trust and confidence is not something that can be taken for granted. *It has to be earned.*

UNDERSTAND THE NEED

Understanding the customer's need is the heart of the sales process. What is learnt here influences what salespeople do in the final two phases. It is here that salespeople discover what is on their customer's minds—problems to be solved, needs to be satisfied and so on. In other words, the customer's reasons for buying.

Additionally, it is possible to learn other things about customers. What can they afford? What factors will influence the buying decision? Who will actually make the decision? Is the customer ready to make a decision? What will influence the customer to buy?

MAKE A RECOMMENDATION

Once your salespeople have a full understanding of what the customer needs and what will motivate them to buy, they are in a position to make a recommendation. When this point is reached, the salesperson can 'test the water' and—if the time seems right—present their recommendation.

The recommendation must be a compelling case for buying, presented from the customer's point of view. It must be presented logically, with conviction and forcefulness that convey a genuine belief in the recommendation that is being made.

COMPLETE THE SALE

As the recommendation is made there are many 'buying signals' that indicate the customer's readiness to say, 'Yes! Where do I sign?'—gestures, smiles, questions, comments and so on. The challenge is to recognize these signals—and ask for the order.

Often, asking for the order is not easy.

You have to ask for the order

- Most of us don't like to hear the answer, 'No!' when we ask for the order, so it can be comfortable not to ask the question, to keep things moving along—and avoid the perceived risk of asking that all-important question.
- Additionally, we don't like to provoke the objections (obstacles) that might arise when asking for the order—because we must then understand them and address them successfully, or risk forfeiting the sale. On the other hand, obstacles are a great way of understanding just where the customer stands and, once they are understood and handled effectively, the sale can be ours for the asking.

At this point in the sales process it is time to complete what we started and what we have worked towards—it is time to complete the sale. During the *complete the sale* phase, it is important to keep these points in mind:

- If your people have moved carefully through the sales process and reached agreement with their customers at each step of the way, they will have *earned the right* to ask for the order
- And if the recommendation reflects their understanding and the agreements reached with the customer, then they stand a very good chance of getting the answer they want.

COMMUNICATION SKILLS

Five communication skills are important to the success of your people's sales efforts. The definitions of each of these are given below, based on those in *The Shorter Oxford English Dictionary*:

- *Listening*   (from the old English *hlysan*) To hear attentively; to give ear to; to pay attention

- *Verifying*   (from the Latin *versus*, true) To prove by good evidence or valid testimony; to show to be true by demonstration or evidence; to ascertain or test the accuracy or correctness of
- *Questioning*   (from the Latin *quaestrio*, seek or inquire) To ask a question or questions of; enquiring or asking
- *Observing*   (from the Latin *observare*, attend to or watch over) To notice, remark, perceive, see a thing or fact; to regard with attention; to watch
- *Explaining*   (from the Latin *planus*, plain) To unfold, to make plain or intelligible; to make oneself understood, speak plainly.

Each of these communication skills is important, to one degree or another, in each of the phases of the sales process—and in executing certain sales skills that are important to the sales process.

Exercise 2—What did the customer say?

This exercise is intended to be used with your people by asking them one by one to repeat to each other (slightly out of earshot) the following message received from a customer. This is a version of the old 'Chinese whispers' exercise for showing people how hard it is to listen. After everyone has heard the message they can discuss what they think they heard. You can start the ball rolling by reading the following statement to one of your team.

The customer's statement

We have a major problem with your company. We're launching a new product next month and our production schedule is in jeopardy because of the key component that you provide. We awarded you a contract a month ago for 10 000 components—the first shipment of which arrived on schedule two days ago. However, 10 of the first 100 'out of the box' failed to meet out specifications. Our production manager, Fred Flemming, said 'With a failure rate that high, it's pointless to test the rest—and another shipment's due in two days!' We need the components—on time and to specifications. You're in trouble! Your major competitor says they can have 5000 up-to-spec components here in three days and the rest within a week.

So . . . can you replace that first shipment—and how fast? What confidence do we have that the remaining components will meet specifications?

Alternatively, you could read the message out to the whole group and after they have heard it ask them to jot down what they have heard; then they can all compare notes.

Having completed this exercise it should be apparent just how hard it is to listen and to recall exactly what was said. To be able to listen attentively to customers is a key selling skill.

SALES SKILLS

The four sales skills covered in this book tend to be applicable at specific points in the sales process. The following are brief descriptions:

The four sales skills are:

■ Building rapport
■ Qualifying opportunities
■ Describing benefits
■ Handling obstacles

■ *Building rapport*   (from the Old French *rapporter*, to refer)
Reference; relationship; connection, correspondence

This skill is especially important in the first phase of the sales process—the time at which salespeople begin earning the right to proceed. Of course, rapport with the customer must be continued, built upon and developed throughout the sales process

■ *Qualifying opportunities*   (from the Latin *qualificare*, of what kind)
To invest with a quality or qualities; to designate in a particular way

In sales, qualifying addresses the basic question, 'Is this a real opportunity to sell?'
– Does the customer have a need? Is the customer interested in what is on offer?
– Is the customer ready to buy?
– Is the customer willing to buy?
– Is the customer able to buy?
– Can the customer's need be satisfied by me?

Positive answers—particularly early in the sales process—help to ensure that time is being spent on sales effort which has a chance of paying off

- *Describing benefits* (from the Latin *benefactum*, good deed) advantage; profit; good; to improve, help forward

    In selling, providing benefit is more than the ability to give advantage. It includes the important concept of demonstrating the ability to give advantage *from the perspective of the customer.* Describing benefits that are *important to the customer* is key to the ability to make recommendations successfully

- *Handling obstacles* (from the Latin *obstare*, in the way) A hindrance, impediment, obstruction; resistance, objection

    Sooner or later—often later, but even better sooner—customers raise obstacles. As we indicated earlier, it is important to remember that obstacles are a great way of understanding just where the customer stands. Once salespeople understand the obstacles and handle them effectively, they can move forward and the sale can be theirs for the asking.

Exercise 3—A quick skills assessment

This assessment is based on what we have covered in this chapter and is intended to give your people the chance to see how they rate their skills before we go further with our learning journey. Get your staff to rate themselves on the following scales, whereby:

7 = comfortable, little need for improvement
4 = so-so, need some improvement
1 = uncomfortable, major need for improvement

Get them to highlight specific areas they want to address and indicate three to five of their highest priorities.

Skill areas	Rating	Specific improvements
Sales process		
■ Earn the right	1 2 3 4 5 6 7	
■ Understand the need	1 2 3 4 5 6 7	
■ Make a recommendation	1 2 3 4 5 6 7	
■ Complete the sale	1 2 3 4 5 6 7	
Communications		
■ Listening	1 2 3 4 5 6 7	
■ Verifying	1 2 3 4 5 6 7	
■ Questioning	1 2 3 4 5 6 7	

- Observing   1 2 3 4 5 6 7
- Explaining   1 2 3 4 5 6 7

Sales

- Building rapport   1 2 3 4 5 6 7
- Qualifying opportunities   1 2 3 4 5 6 7
- Describing benefits   1 2 3 4 5 6 7
- Handling obstacles   1 2 3 4 5 6 7

CONCLUSION

This first chapter has aimed to give a flavour of the content of this book and has, we hope, given you an indication of the learning journey you are about to embark on with your people. As the journey unfolds there will be examples of effective selling in action, as well as exercises for you to use to help you to guide your staff's learning. Selling effectively is hard to demonstrate away from the reality and pressure of face-to-face meetings with customers. However, as far as is possible this book will help you to improve the sales performance of your team.

PART 1

COMMUNICATION SKILLS

In this part of the book we are going to focus on the importance of communication skills in the sales process.

KEY LEARNING POINTS

The following are the key learning points that will be covered in the three chapters in Part 1:

- Understand the idea of 'active listening'

- Be able to apply listening and verifying skills throughout the sales process

- Understand about observing and questioning

- Be able to apply appropriate observing and questioning skills for the 'earn the right' and the 'understand the need' phases of the sales process

- Be able to apply the skill of explaining in the sales process

All of this learning is intended to be applied directly to the sales process, though communication skills are of course of much wider value than this. By focusing in this way it is possible to emphasize certain ways in which communication skills can directly improve sales performance. It is helpful if you can get your staff to look at how they can 'target' their sales effort so that the value of communication skills becomes clear.

Exercise 4—Targeting your sales efforts

In the space overleaf identify at least two different sales situations in which you meet customers. These could differ in the location, the amount of time spent with them, the degree of formality, and so on.

Then identify the typical customers you meet in these situations. Use whatever criteria you think appropriate for describing these customers.

Sales situations	Customers

We will use this work later.

CHAPTER 2

*L*ISTENING AND VERIFYING

KEY LEARNING POINTS

- **Understand the idea of active listening**
- **Know the six steps to success in active listening**
- **Be able to apply listening, verifying and active listening skills throughout the sales process**

INTRODUCTION

Listening is key to success from the beginning of the sales process to its end—a point that scarcely needs to be laboured. Verifying is equally important and goes hand in hand with effective listening. Often what we think we have heard is not, in fact, what we should have heard. The exercise in the previous chapter should have reinforced this point. The importance and use of listening and verifying skills in the sales process is shown in Figure 2.1.

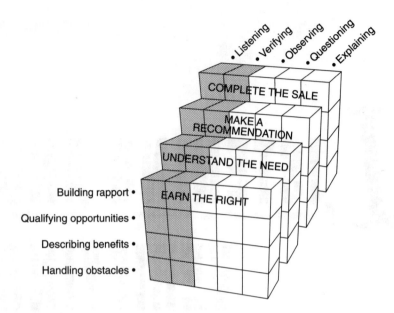

FIGURE 2.1: Listening and verifying: Overview

Source: Miller, H., *The ASTD Trainer's Sourcebook: Sales Training*, McGraw-Hill New York, 1995, p. 367

ACTIVE LISTENING: WHAT AND HOW

Active listening is the combination of two key communication skills, listening and verifying. When you and your team practise active listening you are doing three things:

- Listening with a purpose
- Listening with undivided attention focused on what is being said—making a conscious effort to hear
- Verifying what you hear as you listen, to ensure understanding.

STEPS TO ACTIVE LISTENING

Here are six steps that are particularly helpful when people are attempting to make active listening one of their 'second nature' behaviours:

Listening actively is critical for building rapport

- Listen attentively
  - Every effort has to be made by people to concentrate on what the other person is saying, not on thinking about what they themselves are going to say next

- People need to be aware of their posture; the right posture enhances our ability to concentrate, it eliminates distractions—and communicates that we are listening attentively
■ Verify understanding
  - The first step is for people to pause and think about what was said, then think about what to say
  - They can then 'reflect back' what they heard using different words—without adding anything
  - Alternatively, they can state what they think the other person meant by what they said. This is more complex because it requires the addition of interpretation and inference—and it requires the other person to respond
■ Get confirmation
  - This is done by asking whether what we think we heard is what the other person meant us to hear. This has to be done by phrasing the question something like, 'Have I got it right, that . . .?'
■ Seek clarification
  - If something is not clear, people should immediately say so and ask for clarification. 'I am sorry, but I don't know what you mean, could you clarify it for me' might be a suitable intervention
■ Assume responsibility
  - No matter how ineffective the other person might be in explaining what they want to say it is important not to blame them for the apparent failure in communication
  - It is important for salespeople to build rapport, making people feel foolish or at fault is not only rude but counterproductive
■ Non-verbal clues
  - People should look for non-verbal clues by maintaining eye contact and being aware of the other person's gestures, posture, movements, and so on.

Listen with your eyes

These six steps will lead to a clarity of understanding and perception that will significantly enhance the rapport that salespeople are seeking to establish. This is particularly true of the first meeting with the customer.

Exercise 5—Learning to listen

In this exercise members of your team play one of three roles; the speaker role; the listener role; the observer role. The aim of the exercise is to practise the skills of listening and verifying. The exercise is intended to reinforce and enhance the point already made about the six steps to 'active listening'.

Active listening:

■ Listen attentively
■ Verify
■ Confirm
■ Clarify
■ Be responsible
■ Watch non-verbals

The facilitator of the exercise needs to think of a topic which is currently of interest to the team.

People taking the speaker role then prepare and deliver an opening statement and talk about the chosen topic. During this stage they respond to any questions posed by the person taking the listener role.

People taking the listener role have the aim of learning about and reaching a clear understanding of what the speaker is saying. To do this listeners should:

■ Look for places to stop the speaker and clarify
■ Be alert for areas that need clarification
■ Ensure they understand
■ Summarize what has been understood.

The following 'listener's tips' will help listeners:

■ Concentrate on the other person
    – pay attention to everything that is said
    – organize the information in your mind, while you listen
    – take notes of key words and phrases
    – maintain eye contact
■ Avoid planning your next comment while the other person is speaking
    – use a pause to collect your throughts before speaking
■ Ask for clarification when you need it
    – take responsibility for your lack of understanding
    – persist until you are clear
■ Focus on what is 'not said' as well as what is said
    – there may be omissions and/or distortions in what you are hearing
    – ask questions and verify to fill the gaps
    – remember the gaps are in your understanding
■ Let the other person talk as long as it is leading somewhere
    – use a question to stop or change direction
    – don't cut the speaker off short.

People taking the observer role have several tasks. First is timing the discussion to last no longer than, say, three minutes. Second is to observe how the listener verified and allowed the speaker to lead the discussion. Third is to use the following assessment guide:

- ■ Behaviours that help
  - – Verifies frequently
  - – Confirms as part of verification
  - – Seeks clarification when needed
  - – Assumes responsibility for misunderstanding
  - – Maintains eye contact
  - – Exhibits attentive body posture
- ■ Behaviours that hinder
  - – Interrupts
  - – Leads the discussion
  - – Fails to seek clarification when needed
  - – Does not reflect back frequently
  - – Places the burden for misunderstanding on the speaker
  - – Exhibits poor non-verbal contact.

When speakers, listeners and observers have completed their roles a group discussion can be held. In this discussion speakers comment on how well they have been understood. Listeners comment on how they found the exercise and observers comment from their assessment sheets. Other members of the group can add their own thoughts about the discussion they have just witnessed.

ACTIVE LISTENING AND THE SALES PROCESS

As the illustration at the start of this chapter indicates, active listening is important in all phases of the sales process. However, there are some particular points at which the power of active listening can make the difference between average and excellent sales performance.

THE FIRST MEETING

It is important at the first meeting to ensure that the customer feels in charge of the discussion and is able to lead it to where they want to go. Salespeople who follow this route and actively listen, paying close attention to the customer, will have a much better initial impact than salespeople who are keen to explain who they are and what they can do for the customer.

IDENTIFYING NEEDS

When customers talk about their business they will sprinkle their conversation with clues about what they want from the person they are talking to. This is not stated explicitly and it requires very concentrated listening to 'hear' the customer's unspoken cries for help.

BUYING SIGNALS

Customers who find that they have an attentive 'listening ear' will often reward the attentiveness with clear information about what, when, how they want to buy and who they want to buy it from. These signals, though clear to the active listener, may be hidden in a veritable waterfall of words.

Exercise 6—Active listening assessment

Listening is an excellent approach for building a good relationship with customers and is a way of expressing genuine interest in the other person.

Using the assessment below ask your team to assess themselves on the following scale:

7 = comfortable, little need for improvement
4 = so-so, need some improvement
1 = uncomfortable, major need for improvement

I . . .	Rating	Specific improvements
■ Verify frequently	1 2 3 4 5 6 7	
■ Do not interrupt	1 2 3 4 5 6 7	
■ Reflect back frequently	1 2 3 4 5 6 7	
■ Confirm as part of verification	1 2 3 4 5 6 7	
■ Avoid leading the discussion	1 2 3 4 5 6 7	
■ Seek clarification when needed	1 2 3 4 5 6 7	
■ Assume responsibility for misunderstanding	1 2 3 4 5 6 7	
■ Maintain eye contact	1 2 3 4 5 6 7	
■ Exhibit an attentive posture	1 2 3 4 5 6 7	

CONCLUSION

At this point we have discussed and practised two skills that are key to success throughout the sales process. We have shown how the skills of 'listening' and 'verifying' can work together as *active listening*—an approach that will contribute to selling success.

CHAPTER 3

OBSERVING AND QUESTIONING

KEY LEARNING POINTS

- **Understand the role and importance of observing and questioning skills in the sales process**
- **Identify the types of information that can be gathered from customers through observing**
- **Understand the use of general questions**
- **Be able to define and use questions in the sales process**
- **Understand the concept of 'buying objectives' and 'buying influences'**
- **Be able to define and use closed and leading questions**
- **Be able to identify and use questions for understanding a customer's need**

INTRODUCTION TO OBSERVING AND QUESTIONING

As with listening and verifying, observing and questioning are key to selling success—from beginning to end of the sales process. However, these skills are especially important early in the sales process—during the 'earn the right' phase. Observing is a valuable way to pick up clues about the customer—especially at the first time of meeting. Properly phrased questions are also important—questions that help to get the customer to 'open up' and talk.

THE OBSERVING SKILL

The observing skill is particularly useful at the beginning of the sales process when salespeople are attempting to 'build rapport'. Observation of customers can tell salespeople a great deal about such customers' current state of mind and reaction to the salesperson. Observations of customers and their environment can also provide information about their long-term behaviour patterns—which is especially important in longer-term sales relationships.

Listen with your eyes

In sales situations, observing involves four steps:

- Look for a clue (or clues) that might suggest certain characteristics or traits in the customer
- Interpret the clues—a particularly important step when drawing conclusions about the customer's longer-term behaviour patterns
- Verify the accuracy of the interpretation—and the presence of the characteristic that salespeople think they have detected
- Use the clues and the interpretation of them—verified of course—to help to build a relationship with the customer and to decide on the next stage.

The importance of observing in the sales process is depicted in Figure 3.1.

Exercise 7—Observing: what you can learn

Get your people to do this exercise individually before meeting as a group to discuss what they come up with.

In the first few seconds of face-to-face meetings with customers they typically provide a lot of non-verbal clues—clues that can tell you a lot about your customers and their current state of mind, *if you observe them*.

Some common 'states of mind' or characteristics are listed down the left side of the chart on pages 26 and 27.

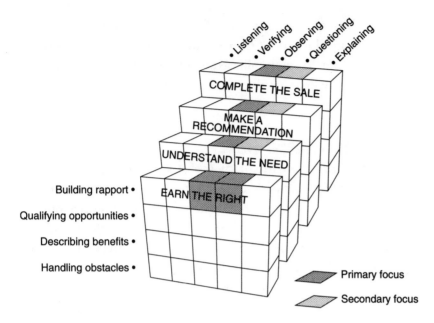

FIGURE 3.1: Observing and questioning: Overview

Source: Miller, H., *The ASTD Trainer's Sourcebook: Sales Training*, McGraw-Hill New York, 1995, p. 369

- Write down clues that you might pick up from your customers that would point to each of those characteristics
- Make notes about how you would interpret each clue
- Then make notes about ways in which you might verify your interpretation—a question, a statement, and so on
- Finally, indicate what you might do as a result of observing that clue.

Characteristic	Clues	Your interpretation	Your verification	Your action
Relaxed				
Tense				

Characteristic	Clues	Your interpretation	Your verification	Your action
Unhurried				
Short of time				
Preoccupied				
Formal				
Detail oriented				

WHAT IMPRESSIONS DO YOU MAKE?

In any situation observing is a two-way street. In sales both salespeople and customers form impressions of each other when they meet. Observing is a powerful skill. When salespeople use this skill properly they can learn a great deal about their customers, just as their customers can learn a great deal about them. It is important for salespeople to know the kind of impression that they make on customers.

It will help your people to focus on the impression they make if you get them to complete the following assessment for themselves.

Exercise 8—The impression I make

Rate yourself on each aspect of the impression you think you make, whereby:

7 = good, little need for improvement
4 = average, need some improvement
1 = poor, major need for improvement

Note specific areas for improvement and then state in an action plan two or three steps you will take to improve your performance

My . . .	Rating	Specific improvements
■ Clothing	1 2 3 4 5 6 7	
■ Personal grooming	1 2 3 4 5 6 7	
■ Speech patterns	1 2 3 4 5 6 7	
■ Posture	1 2 3 4 5 6 7	
■ Gestures	1 2 3 4 5 6 7	
■ Eye contact	1 2 3 4 5 6 7	
■ Surroundings	1 2 3 4 5 6 7	

INTRODUCTION TO QUESTIONING

Early in a sales meeting it is important to avoid asking questions which can be answered by a single word—especially 'No'. Such questions are called closed questions because the single word answer effectively 'closes' the enquiry, and sometimes the whole meeting. Later we will look at using closed questions to help to 'close' the sale. However, the aim at the beginning is to open the conversation and to get the customer to speak.

Skilful use of questioning is especially important in the *'understanding the need'* phase of the sales process. Learning about a customer's buying objectives and buying influences is the main task during this phase, and questioning—accompanied by listening and verifying—is the main tool to use.

BUYING OBJECTIVES AND INFLUENCES

Customers are there because they have a problem to solve, they have a need to satisfy, they want help with their buying decision. Salespeople are there to answer these needs and to provide the help

Salespeople still have to 'earn the right' through building rapport which the customer wants. It is imperative, therefore, that salespeople understand the problem that must be solved or the need that must be satisfied—before they can make a sound recommendation and then complete the sale.

When salespeople work with their customers to make a sale—and, therefore, help them to buy—there are two areas that have to be fully understood.

- *Buying objectives*   What the customer wishes to accomplish
- *Buying influences*   Factors which will influence the customer's buying decision.

Buying objectives are those reasons—problems to solve, needs to satisfy—that bring the customer to the sales situation. Consider these examples.

- A customer comes into a camera shop to buy a new camera. She is going on holiday in a week's time—her old camera is broken and is not worth repairing. This customer has a problem to solve
- Another customer comes into the camera shop to buy a new camera. However, this customer has last year's model; it is perfectly good but the new model has a number of advanced features that make it this year's leading-edge camera in its class. This customer has a need to satisfy.

The distinction between having a problem and having a need is not necessarily clear-cut. However, in these examples, needs that must be satisfied tend to have a strong emotional component to them—as with the person who 'must have this year's camera'.

Of course, some people wish to buy a product or service for a combination of reasons. Consider a medical researcher who must travel to Paris to present the results of an important study. She goes to a travel agent to buy tickets to Paris. She has a problem to solve—getting to Paris. The study is so important that the presentation in Paris could 'make' her career. Therefore, there is also a need to be satisfied—less objective and concrete, definitely more emotional in nature than simply getting to Paris.

Whatever motivates customers, they have reasons for buying—their buying objectives—which salespeople must understand to be successful in their selling efforts.

BUYING INFLUENCES

In addition to understanding buying objectives it is also important to understand customers' buying influences—those factors that will tip their buying decision towards a particular product or service. Some of these influences are quite logical, straightforward and objective in nature:

- Does the product or service meet the customer's requirements?
- Is the price acceptable? Does it fit within the customer's budget?
- Will the product or service be available when the customer wants it?
- If others are involved in the decision, will they approve the purchase?
- Does the customer have specific expectations for the product or service that are longer term in nature—warranty, ongoing support, and so on?

Other buying influences are less objective, less easily explained— more emotional, more subjective in nature:

- Does the customer like the product or service?
- Does the customer like or feel comfortable with the salesperson?
- Is the salesperson believed and trusted by customers to meet their requirements, expectations, and so on?

Learning about buying objectives and buying influences is a major step in understanding the customer's needs—and ultimately in completing the sale. *Successful salespeople* will:

Asking the right questions and listening actively with eyes and ears is the way to discover this vital information

- Understand the factors that motivate customers to buy from them
- Be able to determine whether the customer is ready, willing and able to buy
- By showing a real interest in customers, continue to build rapport
- With the rapport that is built *earn the right to continue their sales efforts.*

Exercise 9—Buying objectives and buying influences

Referring back to Exercise 4, each member of your team identified sales situations and customers. Using this as a basis, ask them to individually prepare a list of buying objectives and buying influences for at least two of their customers.

Customer	Buying objectives	Buying influences

TYPES OF QUESTIONS

Questions serve two broad functions in working towards an understanding of the customer's need and ultimately in completing the sale—to open up the discussion and to focus it. As shown in Figure 3.2, there are three types of questions that are useful in this 'open up–focus in' scheme:

■ General questions, also known as open questions, are used to open up the discussion
■ Specific and closed questions are used to focus in
■ Leading questions can serve either purpose.

GENERAL (OPEN) QUESTIONS

General questions are useful throughout the sales process, whenever there is a need to probe and gather information from the customer:

Open questions help to gather information

■ General questions typically begin with *what?*, *how?*, *who?*, *why?*, *when?* and *where?*

31

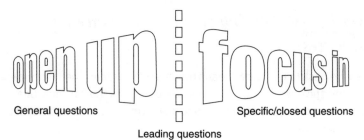

General questions   Specific/closed questions

Leading questions

FIGURE 3.2: Types of questions

Source: Miller, H., *The ASTD Trainer's Sourcebook: Sales Training,* McGraw-Hill New York, 1995, p. 230

- Because such questions are difficult to answer in one or two words they cause people to open up and talk
- In addition they allow salespeople to expand the dialogue they are having with the customer by directing the discussion towards areas that are of interest to the sales effort.

These questions are particularly useful early in a sales effort. In the very early stages the last thing that salespeople wish to do is to give the customer the opportunity to answer a question with one or two words—in particular the dreaded 'No'.

SPECIFIC/CLOSED QUESTIONS

As salespeople talk with their customers there are times when they need brief, short, to-the-point answers:

- For a specific piece of information
- To verify and confirm understanding
- To focus the conversation and reach some sort of conclusion
- To re-focus the conversation if it seems to be drifting away from the business in hand.

Closed questions help to clarify and confirm

Questions that serve this purpose are referred to as specific questions. When specific questions request a 'yes' or 'no' answer they are often referred to as closed questions. As with general questions, specific and closed questions are useful throughout the sales process—whenever it is necessary to temporarily stop gathering information and bring focus to the information that has already been gathered.

LEADING QUESTIONS

Occasionally it is necessary to point customers in a particular direction—a direction that will provide new information in areas of specific interest to the sales effort:

- To stimulate thinking in new directions ('What would happen if ... ?')
- To cause the customer to evaluate the consequences of not acting ('What would happen if you didn't ... ?')
- To force a reply that supports the sales effort ('So you think it would be wise to ... ?')
- To force a choice in order to help guide the discussion in the right direction ('Do you prefer ... ?')

Questions that perform these functions are referred to as leading questions. Note that leading questions can either *open up* the discussion, or *focus in* the discussion—depending on the salesperson's purpose at a specific point in time. The first two questions above *open up* the discussion, and the second two *focus in* the discussion.

TIPS ON QUESTIONING

'Open up—Focus in'

- Ask questions that help to gather the information needed
  - use general questions to get people to open up and talk
  - use specific questions to focus the conversation, reach conclusions, and so on
  - use leading questions to get a specific answer or to move the conversation in a specific direction
  - avoid closed questions early in the sales effort
- Listen to the answers to the questions
  - focus on what the customer is saying
  - don't formulate the next question if the customer is talking
- Use a deliberate line of questioning to go in the direction that supports the sales effort
  - determine the information needed to reach the goal of completing the sale
  - use a mix of general, specific/closed, and leading questions to gather information and keep the discussion on track

- check that the information gathered and the customer's response is appropriate; if not, adjust the line of questioning accordingly
- the sales meeting is not an interrogation. Customers do not like being grilled.

Scenario 1—The coffee maker

The scene is a large electrical retailer where a salesperson and a customer are talking. They have chatted briefly and the salesperson has heard the customer say that they are looking for a coffee maker.

Salesperson	So, you're interested in buying a coffee maker?
Customer	Yes, that's right.
Salesperson	Could you give me an idea of how you plan to use it; at home, or in the office?
Customer	I want it for the office and it needs to be reliable because it will take quite a bashing.
Salesperson	So you want a high quality machine?
Customer	Well, yes, within limits; my budget won't stretch too far.
Salesperson	What price are you thinking of paying?
Customer	Oh, about £40.
Salesperson	And you just want one machine, do you?
Customer	Well, no, I want between 10 and 12 machines.
Salesperson	So this is an important choice for you. You don't want to buy a machine that people will be critical of?
Customer	No way. I don't want the staff blaming me for problems to do with the coffee maker, being a mess, breaking down and so on.
Salesperson	It seems to me that we have to think seriously about the top of the range models for robustness and reliability, do you agree?

Customer	Well, yes, but I have to watch the cost.
Salesperson	OK, what other requirements do you have for the machine?
Customer	It needs to have a non-spill device for when people take the pot off during the cycle.
Salesperson	OK, anything else?
Customer	It needs to have capacity for 12–15 cups per cycle and it has to be easy to fill, easy to clean, have a permanent filter or disposable ones that are easy to fit and easily replaceable.
Salesperson	Well, that's quite a list and I'm sure we can provide what you want, but I think the price is going to be nearer £50 than £40. Can you stretch your budget that far?
Customer	That might be possible, if you can provide exactly what I want.
Salesperson	Then I think we should take a look at the Sensa-Java Turo 12 coffee maker.

Exercise 10—A questioning demonstration

This exercise works best if you ask your team to read the scenario and complete the observer's sheet before they talk to each other. Here is a suggestion for how you can introduce the exercise to your team.

In Scenario 1 the salesperson has used a questioning approach to establish the customer's objectives and buying influences. Read the scenario again and complete the 'observer's sheet' provided below. When you have done this discuss your thoughts with your group.

Questioning skill	Comment
Effective use of questions ■ general ■ specific/closed ■ leading	
Organized questions in a logical, productive sequence	

Questioning skill	Comment
Verified understanding ■ rephrased or interpreted, did not repeat verbatim ■ confirmed understanding	
Observed the customer ■ verified observations	
Listened actively to the customer	
Let the customer talk, did not monopolize the discussion	
Learned about the customer's ■ buying objectives ■ buying influences	
General comments	

COMMENTS ON THE QUESTIONING TECHNIQUE

The questioning technique demonstrated in Exercise 9 has the distinct advantage, if it is done properly, of giving customers the impression that salespeople are interested in them, their problems and their needs. When customers have this feeling they usually provide any information that they think will help the salesperson to help them. So they respond well to the questioning approach as long as the salesperson does not *take the control of the discussion away from the customer.*

Active listening

The danger with the questioning approach is that used carelessly (without care) it can lead customers to the impression that the only aim salespeople have is to help themselves. When customers pick up this impression they will try to close the discussion as soon as possible.

Customers make the decision *not to buy* much more quickly than they make the decision to buy. From the very beginning of the

It is usually easier for customers to decide *not to buy*

sales meeting the aim should be to allow the customer to grow increasingly confident that they want to buy from this salesperson who they feel is focusing on *helping* them meet their needs.

Exercise 11—*Assessing my questioning technique*

Ask each of your staff to assess themselves using the following assessment sheet.

Rate yourself on each of the techniques:

7 = comfortable, little need for improvement
4 = so-so, need some improvement
1 = poor, major need for improvement

Note specific areas of improvement against each tecnhnique and identify two or three action steps you can take to improve your performance.

I . . .	Rating	Specific improvements
■ Use general questions to 'open up' customers	1 2 3 4 5 6 7	
■ Use specific/closed questions to 'focus in'	1 2 3 4 5 6 7	
■ Use leading questions to direct customers' thinking and comments	1 2 3 4 5 6 7	
■ Use active listening	1 2 3 4 5 6 7	
■ Verify my understanding	1 2 3 4 5 6 7	
■ Organize questions into a productive sequence	1 2 3 4 5 6 7	
■ Successfully gather the information I need	1 2 3 4 5 6 7	

CONCLUSION

Observing and questioning are skills which take some time, practice and experience to develop. There is a balance between gathering information in a friendly, helpful way and interrogation. One way to do this is to invite the customer to participate by using open questions to *open up*, and more specific/closed questions to *focus in* and to gain agreement to information that is reflected back.

In addition, if the needs of the customer are re-stated and confirmed from time to time during the questioning customers begin to believe that the salesperson is focusing on them and their needs. This makes them feel comfortable with and in charge of the process; they are buying not being sold to, and this is an important distinction.

CHAPTER 4

*E*XPLAINING

KEY LEARNING POINTS

- **Understand the role and importance of the explaining skill**
- **Know the characteristics of an explanation**
- **Be able to use explaining skills in a sales situation**

INTRODUCTION TO EXPLAINING

Although the explaining skill can be useful throughout the sales process, it is particularly useful during the last two phases (see Figure 4.1):

- When presenting a recommendation in the 'make a recommendation' phase
- When handling obstacles, typically in the 'complete the sale' phase, and any time there is a need to answer a question.

When there is a need to make a recommendation or to handle obstacles it is necessary to explain well. This means paying attention to the characteristics of a good explanation, which are:

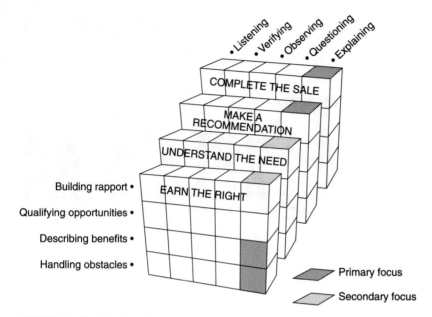

FIGURE 4.1: Explaining: Overview

Source: Miller, H., *The ASTD Trainer's Sourcebook: Sales Training*, McGraw-Hill New York, 1995, p. 374

- Simple language containing no technical jargon
- Short and to the point
- Logical, clear transitions from one point to the next
- Credible, yet dynamic, vivid, exciting for the customer
- Focused on customer objectives.

EXPLAINING

> *explaining* (from the Latin *planus*, plain) To unfold, to make plain or intelligible; to make oneself understood; to speak plainly

Explaining is an essential part of the sales process. When presenting a recommendation the aim is to reach a point where it is easy and natural to ask for the order. When handling obstacles (or answering a question) the need is to clarify and address an issue or concern that the customer has (or to provide information that the customer has requested).

To achieve these aims it is necessary to organize the content, probably while using a 'thinking on your feet' approach. It is only necessary to include the information which directly serves the purpose of the explanation. The key points should be in a logical order, particularly from the customer's point of view. Only add the minimum of necessary detail, take the minimum amount of time and keep the explanation clear and explicit.

Cover complicated explanations in brief 'chunks' and check that the customer has understood and is ready to move on, and in fact does want to hear more. While salespeople are explaining and customers are silent it is not possible to learn about them or how they are reacting to the explanation. Involve customers as much as possible in the explanation.

SUCCESSFUL EXPLANATIONS

Successful explanations:

- Use simple language
- Avoid jargon (unless the customer wants to hear it)
- Keep the explanation short and to the point
- Make sure the explanation is logical
- Provide clear links from one point to the next
- Are credible and concrete
- Are vivid and dynamic, but the salesperson should not overdo it
- Remain focused on the purpose of the explanation and the customer's objectives
- Do not fake answers. The salesperson should say something like, 'I will need to get back to you on that one'. Then find out the answer and get back.

Scenario 2—The coffee maker—continued

The sales meeting we visited in Scenario 1 continues here as the salesperson moves to giving an explanation about the Sensa-Java Turbo 12 coffee maker.

Salesperson   The Sensa-Java Turbo 12 is the nearest machine we have to what you want. It meets all the

	criteria we have discussed and is one of the best machines for its price on the market.
Customer	And how much is it?
Salesperson	It retails at £52 complete with a full two-year guarantee and a spare chromium steel filter. Of course, there will be a quantity discount for you if you buy 10 or more.
Customer	How much discount?
Salesperson	I can do you a deal of £47.50 each for 10 or more; is that acceptable to you?
Customer	It might be; tell me more about the machine's reliability.
Salesperson	It has several features which make it the leading choice of commercial customers. The main ones are the unbreakable coffee pot; auto-shut off when the pot is empty; the non-spill coffee basket; the energy control for efficiency. As you can probably see, it meets all your needs.
Customer	And the capacity?
Salesperson	It is rated as a 12-cup machine.
Customer	And what colours is it available in. I notice this one is white.
Salesperson	I'm not sure of the full range, but I'll check for you.

In this scenario the salesperson has attempted to explain the product which seems to best meet the customer's needs. In the process of doing this the salesperson includes a question which seeks to move the customer towards completing (closing) the sale. This is a legitimate approach to test the customer's readiness to buy and the explanation stage is a good time to try a 'buying signal question'.

Exercise 12—Demonstration of explaining

We suggest that you bring your team together to study the scenario and to discuss the effectiveness of the salesperson's explanation. An alternative, or additional, approach might be to set up a role play with your team using a situation which relates more closely with your own working environment. This can be effective and great fun, as long as the members of the team who role play are not criticized for their performances.

In the second 'coffee maker' scenario the salesperson has explained the product that seems to be the best fit to the customer's needs. Comment on the effectiveness of the explanation using the following 'observer's sheet'. When you have done this discuss your comments with the group.

Explaining skill	Comment
Used simple language, avoided jargon	
Kept the explanation short and to the point: ■ key points in a logical order ■ clear links between points	
Made the explanation credible and concrete	
Made the explanation vivid and dynamic	
Remained focused on the purpose of the explanation	
Didn't attempt to fake answers to questions	
General comments	

Exercise 13—Assessing my explaining skills

This is an assessment for individual members of your team to complete to give them some idea of areas where they might want to improve their performance.

Rate yourself on each of the techniques:

7 = comfortable, little need for improvement

4 = so-so, need some improvement

1 = poor, major need for improvement

Note the specific areas for improvement and identify two or three steps you will take to improve your performance.

I . . .	Rating	Specific improvements
■ Use simple language	1 2 3 4 5 6 7	
■ Avoid jargon, unless it is appropriate	1 2 3 4 5 6 7	
■ Keep the explanation short and to the point	1 2 3 4 5 6 7	
■ Make the explanation logical	1 2 3 4 5 6 7	
■ Provide clear links	1 2 3 4 5 6 7	
■ Make it credible and and concrete	1 2 3 4 5 6 7	
■ Make it vivid and dynamic	1 2 3 4 5 6 7	
■ Stay focused on the purpose of the explanation	1 2 3 4 5 6 7	
■ Stay focused on the customer's objectives	1 2 3 4 5 6 7	
■ Don't 'fake' answers	1 2 3 4 5 6 7	

CONCLUSION

Explaining is a skill which requires salespeople to reach a balance between saying too little and saying too much. Perhaps the best approach is to explain the product or service in small steps, inviting the customer to participate by introducing well–placed questions in the explanation. In this way customers feel that the explanation is being given in direct relationship with what they want to know so they feel in control of the buying decision.

Too many salespeople talk too much and sell too little.

PART 2

EARNING THE RIGHT

KEY LEARNING POINTS

The following are the key learning points that will be covered in the two chapters in Part 2:

■ Understand the importance of the 'earn the right' phase of the sales process

■ Understand the role of key communication skills in this phase

■ Understand the concept of building rapport

■ Be able to apply techniques for building rapport

■ Be able to apply approaches for beginning sales efforts

Introduction to the 'Earn the Right' Phase

The 'earn the right' phase is when salespeople have their first meeting with customers. During this initial interaction both salespeople and customers register their 'first impressions'. This is the time when salespeople have to 'earn the right' to proceed by building a basic level of trust and confidence that encourages customers to stay with the process and grant the salesperson the right to move forward with the sales effort. Such a level of trust and confidence is not something that can be taken for granted; *it has to be earned.*

The skill of building rapport (Chapter 5) is particularly important during this phase. It involves the key communication skills of observing and questioning, in particular:

■ Looking for clues to the customer's characteristics
■ Interpreting those clues and drawing conclusions
■ Verifying the interpretation
■ Using what is learnt to build a relationship with the customer.

The information gained from the observation of the customer during the first few minutes of the initial meeting helps in the formulation of questions which increase the information salespeople have for moving forward; particularly the asking of general (open) questions to get customers to *open up*.

Through listening actively to the answers customers give, salespeople can develop and understand their customers' buying objectives and buying influences which is a great help in beginning the sale (Chapter 6).

CHAPTER 5

*B*UILDING

RAPPORT

KEY LEARNING POINTS

- **Understand the role of key communication skills in building rapport**
- **Understand the concept of building rapport**
- **Be able to apply techniques for building rapport**

INTRODUCTION TO BUILDING RAPPORT

Imagine a situation where a salesperson and a customer have met for the first time. The salesperson wants to accomplish a number of things at this crucial moment. Some of these might be:

Active listening

- Make customers comfortable in the sales situation
- Gain the attention of customers and find out why they are here, thus gaining a sense of the customer's needs
- Ensure that the sales effort can continue beyond this opening moment.

These are short-term objectives for building rapport. Longer-term objectives might include:

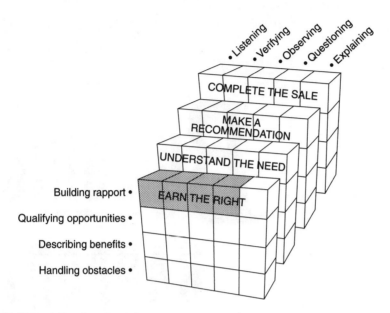

FIGURE 5.1: Earning the right

Source: Miller, H., *The ASTD Trainer's Sourcebook: Sales Training,* McGraw-Hill New York, 1995, p. 376

- Ensure that the customer stays (and will return if necessary), thus enabling the sales process to continue
- Begin to create a dialogue with the customer
- Begin to build a sense of *relationship, agreement and harmony* with the customer.

Building rapport is part of a continuing process of learning about the problems and needs of customers and responding so that customers feel they are being helped and find it easy to make their buying decisions. In Figure 5.1 it is possible to see how building rapport calls upon the key communication skills of listening, verifying, observing and questioning. Of course, all these skills have to have a direction to be effective at this crucial stage in the sales process.

Observing and questioning

BUILDING RAPPORT: THE RIGHT DIRECTION

During the early part of the meeting the primary aim is to achieve a sense of relationship, agreement and harmony. Without this there is no basis for a continuing dialogue. The steps for achieving this sense of relationship, agreement and harmony depend on the particular circumstances, but will probably include the following:

- Acting relaxed and at ease
  - Breathing slowly and deeply, smiling and being welcoming
  - Introducing yourself in a friendly informal way
- Making the other person feel comfortable
  - Using 'small talk' of a personal nature
  - Referring to topics of previous meetings if this is not the first meeting
  - Responding to the customer's comments and not 'taking over' the direction of the conversation
- Listening to the other person
  - Concentrating on what the customer is saying and reacting appropriately with words, gestures, posture, and so on
  - Making a 'conscious effort' to hear
- Getting down to business *when the customer is ready*
  - Watching for clues to when the customer is ready to do business, such as fidgeting, clock watching, direct comments
  - There is usually some clear signal that the 'small talk' is over, but if there are any doubts then a question might clear the air; 'Are we ready to talk about . . . ?' might be sufficient
- Being aware of non-verbal behaviours
  - Facing the customer 'eye to eye'
  - Establishing eye contact and maintaining it without staring
  - Using an informal and friendly posture avoids customers reacting defensively
  - Being receptive to what the customer says and does without smothering or being intimidating
- Projecting a positive image
  - Dressing and grooming appropriately for the particular circumstances of the sales situation
  - If the meeting is on your home ground be sure the surroundings project the image that serves the sales process.

With this approach it is likely that customers will feel at ease and be able to talk easily and freely about themselves and their needs, which is the whole purpose of this first stage of building rapport.

Active listening

Observation

Scenario 3—The customer from hell

All salespeople fear meeting the 'customer from hell'. There are very few of these people about, but meeting them even on the odd occasion can severely damage a salesperson's confidence. Our scenario takes place in the office of the customer from hell, who we will call Mr Denzel (his first name is Damien, which he very rarely uses). The salesperson is Jack Squires.

Jack has responded to an enquiry from the company purchasing department and he has been passed on to Mr Denzel, who is the production director.

Mr Denzel	Enter.
Jack	[Opening the door and walking confidently in] Good morning, Mr Denzel, I'm ...
Mr Denzel	What's good about it. Sit down. Right you've got five minutes to tell me what you can do for me.
Jack	OK, well I had better get straight down to business.
Mr Denzel	Good.
Jack	Why have you invited me to be here today?
Mr Denzel	Because your brochure said you make the best quality castings, and that's what we need.
Jack	Can you tell me exactly what type of castings you need?

[Picking up a file, Mr Denzel extracts some technical specifications and bangs them down on his desk in front of Jack.]

Mr Denzel	These specifications provide all you want to know. What I want is for you to study these and give me your best price. How long will it take you?
Jack	Thank you. These look very detailed and comprehensive; I'm not used to getting such good information.

[Jack notices the very slightest of smiles flicker across Mr Denzel's face, and then it is gone.]

Mr Denzel   Well?

Jack   I will need to examine these more carefully. Perhaps I can do that and get back to you?

Mr Denzel   I need an answer from you today.

Jack   Do you have an office, or somewhere I can sit to study the specs? If you do, I can give you an answer in about half an hour.

[Jack notices the flicker of a smile again.]

Mr Denzel   Right you can use my secretary's office next door.

[He picks up the phone and presses the key pad.]

Mr Denzel   Jenny, I want you to make room for . . . [Turning to Jack] What's your name . . . ?

Jack   Jack Squires.

Mr Denzel   . . . Jack Squires. He is going to study some specifications.

[He puts the phone down and looks at Jack.]

Mr Denzel   Right, well off you go. Jenny can ring through when you're ready.

In this scenario in spite of the apparent formality, rudeness and directness, Jack has begun to build a rapport with the 'customer from hell'. He is doing it using his communication skills and his understanding of exactly which stage of the sales process he is at.

Exercise 14—Reacting to customers

I suggest you ask your staff to individually read Scenario 3 and to then note down how they think Jack has started to build rapport with Mr Denzel and what skills he has used to do it. Bring them together for a group discussion.

REACTING TO CUSTOMERS

Many salespeople develop an approach, we might call it a style, which they rely on. This happens because they bring their own personality and individuality to bear on all they learn from training and experience. This combination of personality, training and experience forms a uniqueness which usually aids the sales process. If, however, salespeople get 'stuck' with their own unique approach it can limit their success. Sometimes the most important skill a salesperson can have is *adaptability*.

Reacting to customers is all about adaptability. In Scenario 3 whatever Jack intended to do and say went by the board when he met 'the customer from hell'. What he did do was to adapt very quickly to Mr Denzel by adopting a down-to-earth 'businesslike' approach to building rapport with his customer. By noticing (observing) the brief smiles as they flicked across his customer's face he was able to verify that his approach was working.

In this brief scenario Jack is displaying his grasp of communication skills, particularly listening, questioning and observing, and his ability to adapt quickly and react to his customer's behaviour.

Building rapport is as much about attunement as it is about technique. Being able to 'tune in' to the customer's wavelength is a critical factor in building rapport successfully and 'tuning in' is all about reception. It is about receiving the customer's messages, both the spoken and the unspoken, and reacting accordingly.

Scenario 4—The sales angel

We are returning to the meeting between Jack Squires and Mr Denzel. Jack has completed his review of the specification and has made a couple of phone calls to his supervisor, Jane Marsh. Jane has told Jack that he can confirm delivery and that he has some scope to negotiate on price. She has also asked Jack to clarify exactly what Mr Denzel wants. He is ready to do business.

Mr Denzel	Come in. Forty minutes, not bad eh! So what can you tell me?
Jack	Well, Mr Denzel, we can produce the castings you need exactly to this specification and I think we can offer you a competitive price.
Mr Denzel	Good, tell me more.
Jack	Well, I need some more information from you so that I can be quite clear about delivery and price.
Mr Denzel	So what do you want to know?
Jack	Well, first what quantity do you want to order?
Mr Denzel	We want a total of 10 000, in monthly deliveries 0f 1500 to start with.
Jack	And what is your acceptable fault tolerance?
Mr Denzel	No more than 0.5 per cent. Doesn't it say that in the specification?
Jack	It probably does; sorry I must have missed it.
Mr Denzel	Anything else you need to know?
Jack	If we are successful in winning your business and we can satisfy you with our quality, will we continue to get your business?
Mr Denzel	If you play ball with me, I'll play ball with you, and after the first contract of 10 000 I'm willing to consider an annual contract of 20 000. But let me down and not only will I not use you again, but I'll make damn sure the word gets out. How does that sound?
Jack	It sounds to me as if we can do business.

[Jack notices the same brief smile flick across Mr Denzel's face.]

BUILDING RAPPORT: CONTINUING THE PROCESS

In this scenario Jack is continuing to build rapport with Mr Denzel. He is beginning to get a less abrasive response from his customer and he is gathering the information he needs to move on in the sales process. He is being careful to track his customer's mood and directness and he is responding in the same way. Even the point about the fault tolerance is dealt with by Jack taking responsibility for not having the information.

Active listening

The sales meeting is developing to the point where Jack is going to be able to explain about his company and to begin negotiating on price. Jack is already anticipating a tough period of negotiation ahead.

From Mr Denzel's point of view we imagine that he feels very much in control and that he is appreciating the way that Jack is responding to him. We can interpret his behaviour in this way because he is answering Jack's questions positively and fully. The last comment he makes in the scenario seems to indicate that the rapport between them is growing, and that he is prepared to continue the sales process with Jack.

Jack has 'earned the right' to continue

Exercise 15—Building rapport assessment

This is an opportunity for you to pause and to ask your staff to assess themselves in terms of how well they believe they can build rapport. Use the following assessment.

This assessment covers key techniques in 'building rapport'. Rate yourself on each technique:

7 = comfortable, little need for improvement
4 = so-so, need some improvement
1 = uncomfortable, major need for improvement

Note specific areas where you think you could improve and make an action note of two or three steps you will take to improve your performance.

I . . .	Rating	Specific improvements
■ Act relaxed and at ease	1 2 3 4 5 6 7	
■ Make the other person feel comfortable	1 2 3 4 5 6 7	
■ Take time before moving into 'business'	1 2 3 4 5 6 7	
– Customer comfort	1 2 3 4 5 6 7	
– Picking up clues	1 2 3 4 5 6 7	
– Customer readiness	1 2 3 4 5 6 7	
■ Listen	1 2 3 4 5 6 7	

■ Am aware of non-verbal   1 2 3 4 5 6 7
  behaviours
    – Eye to eye   1 2 3 4 5 6 7
    – Friendly posture   1 2 3 4 5 6 7
    – Receptiveness   1 2 3 4 5 6 7
■ Project a positive image
    – Grooming   1 2 3 4 5 6 7
    – Environment   1 2 3 4 5 6 7

CONCLUSION

Building rapport is a continuing process with short- and long-term objectives. The short-term focus is on ensuring that the interaction with the customer is one where both parties feel comfortable and relaxed with each other. The longer-term focus is the building of a dialogue that effectively begins the sales process and earns the salesperson the right to continue.

CHAPTER 6

BEGINNING A SALE

KEY LEARNING POINTS

- **Be able to begin the sale effectively**
- **Know the right point at which to begin the sale**

BEGINNING A SALE

There is a point early in the 'earn the right' phase of the sales process, during the 'building rapport' stage where there are signals that indicate the beginning of the sale. These signals are often half hidden in the conversation and need to be identified by very careful observation and listening. Some people who work as professional buyers are very good at trying not to give these signals until they are ready to move into the buying phase themselves. The attentive salesperson can spot these signals and use them to move the sales process forward.

Active listening

If you study Scenarios 3 and 4 there are several signals, particularly in Scenario 4. Signals are usually, but not always, noticed when customers refer to what they *want* or *need*. And when they ask questions about quality, reliability, delivery and price. Sometimes simply answering these questions directly begins the sales process, but more often the signals can best be used by asking clarifying questions which move directly into 'beginning a sale'.

Exercise 16—Watching for the signals and knowing what to do

This exercise will call for two additional sales situations and customer details to be added to the 'Targeting your sales efforts' sheet that we worked on in Exercise 4. When these two new situations have been identified by each of your staff, proceed with this exercise.

In this 'targeting your sales efforts' activity you will develop approaches for recognizing signals and beginning a sale:

- Look at the sales situations you have identified for this exercise
- Describe each situation briefly
- State what you must do or accomplish in order to begin the sale successfully
- Describe your approach to beginning the sale, that is, how you will know when to begin; and the skills you will use including: observing, questioning, listening, rapport building
- Indicate your reason for selecting this approach.

	Situation 1	Situation 2
Description of the situation		
What you must do or accomplish		
Your approach: ■ observing ■ questioning ■ listening ■ rapport building		

	Situation 1	Situation 2
The reasons for this approach		

Following the completion of the first part of the exercise, open a group discussion about what people have suggested would be the way that they might approach their customers. This discussion should be seen as a learning opportunity that enables everyone to offer their own creative approach to beginning a sale.

Scenario 5—An angel in disguise

In this scenario we again return to see how Jack is getting on with the 'customer from hell', who may not be as bad as he seems.

Mr Denzel OK. So how long would it take you to produce me a prototype casting?

Jack If we can reach an 'agreement in principle' we can have the patterns made and a prototype with you for quality testing in a week, and we will fully offset the cost of this against your subsequent order.

Mr Denzel Hey now. Hang on a minute. I didn't say anything about paying you to produce a prototype.

Jack That's true. But surely you can't expect me to go to the expense of producing a prototype without any assurance of a contract?

Mr Denzel Why not? Your competitors are willing to do just that to get our business.

Jack OK. It will cost us £1000 to produce a prototype and you know as well as I do that we have to recover this cost in our price.

> **Mr Denzel** Yes, I realize that.
>
> **Jack** And if we are to do business together my company need to be able to make a fair profit; you would agree with that wouldn't you?
>
> **Mr Denzel** Yes. I can't argue with you there.
>
> **Jack** So, why don't we agree to pay £500 each for the prototype so that we share the risk, and that way I am sure we can sharpen up our price.
>
> [The smile hovered for a moment longer this time on Mr Denzel's face.]
>
> **Mr Denzel** I like your style, young fellow. What was your name again?
>
> **Jack** Jack . . . Jack Squires.
>
> **Mr Denzel** Right then, Jack, let's have a cup of coffee and get down to business.

PACING THE PROCESS

This ability to go at the customer's pace is known as 'tracking' and is important in allowing customers to feel in control

The beginning of a sale needs to be paced at the speed the customer wants to go at. In Scenario 5 Jack is moving at Mr Denzel's pace. He is not trying to rush forward to clinch a deal. He is exploring the basis of his customer's needs. He is letting his customer dictate the pace of the sales process.

Get customers into the habit of saying 'Yes!'.

In addition, Jack is doing one of the most crucial things of the 'beginning a sale' stage, which is that he is getting Mr Denzel to say 'yes' to some of his suggestions. On two occasions Jack talks about realistic ways of doing business that a 'hard' practical customer like Mr Denzel can only really agree with. This increases the rapport, moves the sales process forward and makes it that little bit easier for Mr Denzel to say 'yes' later in the process when Jack makes his recommendation. Jack has certainly earned his right to continue.

Exercise 17—Earning the right assessment

This exercise is to allow members of your team to assess their own ability to 'earn the right'.

You should rate yourself for each of the listed behaviours on the scale:

7 = comfortable, little need for improvement
4 = so-so, need some improvement
1 = uncomfortable, major need for improvement

Note specific areas for improvement and identify two or three ways that you will take action to improve your performance.

I . . .	Rating	Specific improvements
■ Act relaxed and at ease	1 2 3 4 5 6 7	
■ Make the other person feel comfortable	1 2 3 4 5 6 7	
■ Take time before moving into business	1 2 3 4 5 6 7	
■ Am aware of my non-verbal behaviours	1 2 3 4 5 6 7	
■ Project a positive image	1 2 3 4 5 6 7	
■ Look for clues that tell me about my customer	1 2 3 4 5 6 7	
■ Interpret and verify the clues	1 2 3 4 5 6 7	
■ Use general (open) questions early in the meeting	1 2 3 4 5 6 7	
■ Avoid closed questions	1 2 3 4 5 6 7	
■ Listen attentively	1 2 3 4 5 6 7	

CONCLUSION

Beginning the sale at the right moment is a great help in 'earning the right' to continue. To barge in too early, or to hang about diffidently will both put the customer off. This is a time when the sales process can be easily closed down prematurely by the customer. It is easier because we are still building rapport and the contact is still tenuous. Great care has to be exercised to spot the exact moment to 'begin the sale'.

PART 3

*U*NDERSTANDING THE NEED

In this part of the book we are going to focus on the importance of the 'understanding the need' phase of the sales process.

KEY LEARNING POINTS

The following are the key learning points that will be covered in the two chapters in Part 3:

- Understand the role and importance of the 'understand the need' phase

- Know what communication skills are needed in this phase

- Understand the concept of 'qualifying opportunities'

- Be able to qualify opportunities

Understanding the Need

In this phase salespeople learn many things about the customer. This information can be divided into general/background information; information about 'buying objectives'; and information about 'buying influences'. It is this information which is used to formulate the best recommendation and as a basis for completing the sale. *This phase can be viewed as the heart of the sales process.*

Perhaps the most important tool for salespeople as they work to understand the customer's needs is questioning. The three question types, general (open), specific/closed and leading all come into play as salespeople choose the best way to discover the secret to the customer's buying decision.

CHAPTER 7

QUALIFYING OPPORTUNITIES

KEY LEARNING POINTS

- **Understand the concept of qualifying opportunities**
- **Be able to qualify opportunities**

INTRODUCTION TO QUALIFYING OPPORTUNITIES

Salespeople can spend a great deal of time chasing 'non-existent' sales because they have not discovered answers to the five 'qualifying questions'. These questions are:

- Does the customer have a *need*?
- Is the customer *ready* to buy?
- Is the customer *willing* to buy?
- Is the customer *able* to buy?
- Am I able to satisfy the customer's need?

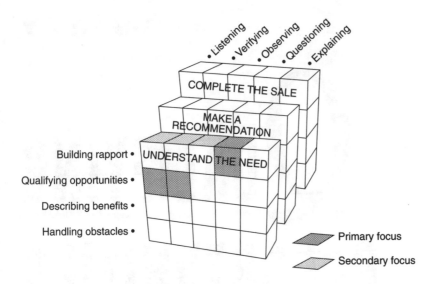

FIGURE 7.1: Understanding the need: Overview

Source: Miller, H., *The ASTD Trainer's Sourcebook: Sales Training*, McGraw-Hill, New York, 1995, p. 378

Discovering answers to these questions involves the first four of the communication skills, with the emphasis on 'questioning'. This is depicted in Figure 7.1.

The first four of our five questions qualify the customer, and the fifth question qualifies the opportunity, given that having qualified the customer it is possible to satisfy their need.

By qualifying opportunities, the time, effort and energy which is invested in the sales process can be focused on those opportunities which are likely to be successful. If opportunities are not qualified then either the effort is wasted, or salespeople could fail to pursue a sale and lose business.

HOW TO QUALIFY OPPORTUNITIES

Salespeople gather information so that they can discover answers to the first four questions about the customer's need, readiness, willingness and ability to buy. To do this salespeople have to call upon all their skills of listening, verifying, observing and especially questioning.

Asking the right questions and actively listening to the answers

It is unlikely that salespeople will ask customers—straight out—if they are 'for real'. Instead this has to be inferred, or not inferred, from the information that is collected. The challenge is for salespeople to reach as sound a conclusion about the opportunity as possible.

Scenario 6—Qualifying the opportunity

In this scenario we return to the meeting between Mr Denzel and Jack Squires. Jenny has brought some coffee and Jack continues.

Jack	Before we 'get down to business', I wonder if I could ask you for some more information?
Mr Denzel	Yes, fire away.
Jack	Why have you decided to approach us at this time? I assume that you have been meeting your needs from some other source up to now?
Mr Denzel	Yes, we have. We have been buying these particular castings from a competitor of yours, and though the quality has been OK we have been having some difficulty with deliveries.
Jack	So delivery is important to you.
Mr Denzel	Yes, it is. We like to operate a tight ship and I don't want to have to carry large stocks.
Jack	It sounds as if you are moving to a 'Just in Time' stock policy.
Mr Denzel	We have a long way to go to reach 'Just in Time' but you're right, that's what we want to achieve if we can.
Jack	Would you be interested in working with us to establish a 'Just in Time' approach? We have an excellent system that does support 'Just in Time'.
Mr Denzel	Yes, we certainly would.
Jack	OK. Now about the quality specification. Our technical people tell me that we can work to your tolerances and that we can provide an

	improved finish. Would you be interested in that?
Mr Denzel	Not if it is going to cost more.
Jack	OK. So really there is a balance here between improving the quality and the cost?
Mr Denzel	Yes, that's it exactly. We have specified the minimum quality we require at the best price. If you can improve on our spec without increasing price, then I'm interested.
Jack	Right. Then finally, what are your payment terms?
Mr Denzel	We pay 60 days from invoice.
Jack	Are you willing to consider different terms?
Mr Denzel	That depends on what they are.
Jack	Well, I'm thinking of how important delivery is to you and I would suggest that you pay us 30 days from delivery date. This will help to make sure that we maintain a regular flow of deliveries.
Mr Denzel	I think we may be able to accommodate you there.

In this scenario Jack has been careful to qualify his customer in terms of the need (which has been Jack's focus for some time in the meeting); the customer's readiness to buy (with the question about previous suppliers); Mr Denzel's willingness to buy (with the question about quality); and then the customer's ability to buy (with the question about payment). Jack has also indicated that his company can satisfy the customer's need (with the suggestions for improved quality and 'Just in Time' systems).

Jack is now moving to a point where he can begin to think about making a recommendation. However, before he is going to be ready to do this he has to make sure that Mr Denzel is ready to listen. One way to do this is to clarify or understand the need in more detail. Before we move on to this stage, I want to explore what happens when the sales opportunity is not qualified in this way.

■ Opening doors
■ Walking away
■ Continuing regardless

WHEN A SALES OPPORTUNITY IS NOT QUALIFIED

When a sales opportunity is not qualified there are three basic alternatives:

■ Salespeople can continue for a short time, hoping to build a bit more rapport with the customer and perhaps leave the door open for future sales activity. This is a good alternative in situations where the customer who is not qualified today—perhaps simply not ready—might well be tomorrow. This option is also useful when the product or service being offered doesn't meet the customer's needs—but might be suitable when needs change.

■ The next advantage is for salespeople to walk away at the earliest moment, thus saving time and effort. If it is a situation in which the opportunity is not qualified because the product or service doesn't meet the customer's needs, then walking away also saves the customer's time and effort; a courtesy that might be remembered by the customer and, as a result, bring the customer back at a later date. Unless the situation is carefully verified this alternative brings with it a greater risk of losing a sale than the first alternative.

■ The third alternative is for the salesperson to press on as far as possible, in the hope of eventually making a sale. This approach minimizes the risk of losing a sale, but the risk of wasting time and effort and alienating the customer increases.

I like to think of these three alternatives as *opening doors*, *walking away* and *continuing regardless*. My own preference is for the 'opening doors' alternative, but this depends on each and every situation. Salespeople have to make a choice as to which approach is appropriate at any one time. Of course, if the steps to qualifying a sale are followed then it should become clear quite early on in the sales process what to do.

Exercise 18—Approaches to qualifying

This exercise is aimed at targeting sales effort by looking at customers identified earlier, or identified now, and then using the following steps for deciding how to approach qualifying them:

- First describe each customer briefly
- Then identify a typical buying objective for each customer
- Indicate what information would be needed to qualify each sales opportunity. This is an important consideration because the information you need will probably not be available unless you ask for it
- Now list the questions you might ask and the observations you might make
- Finally, indicate how you would evaluate whether the opportunity is qualified, based on the information you gather.

	Customer 1	Customer 2
Description of the customer		
Typical buying objective		
Information you need to qualify		
How you will gather the information		
How you will evaluate the information		

THE VALUE OF QUALIFYING OPPORTUNITIES

There are four particularly valuable activities that take place during the process of qualifying sales opportunities. They are each of benefit to the salesperson. They are:

- *Focusing* time and effort where it has the best chance of resulting in a sale
- *Consolidating* the need that the customer has, so that any subsequent recommendation can be presented in a way that precisely meets the customer's needs
- *Impressing* the customer with the highly professional approach that has been taken during the early stages of the sales process
- *Ensuring* that the sales process has a chance of ending in a 'win–win' situation, where both the salesperson and the customer are happy and satisfied with the outcome.

Keeping the customer in the driving seat

One of the hidden values of qualifying sales opportunities, that arises when all of the above are taken together, is the way in which customers feel that they are in command of the process and that it is their 'buying needs' which are driving the sale, rather than the needs of the salesperson. For a buyer to leave a sales meeting with the sense that they have made a good 'buying decision' is the sign of a truly professional salesperson.

Exercise 19—A qualifying assessment

In this exercise the idea is for your staff to rate themselves in terms of their qualifying skills on a scale of:

7 = comfortable, little need for improvement
4 = so-so, need some improvement
1 = uncomfortable, major need for improvement

I . . .	Rating	Specific improvements
■ Use questioning, listening and verifying skills to qualify opportunities	1 2 3 4 5 6 7	

- Use my observing skill   1 2 3 4 5 6 7
  in qualifying
- Use and assess the   1 2 3 4 5 6 7
  information I gather
- Qualify opportunities   1 2 3 4 5 6 7
  quickly
- Recognize situations   1 2 3 4 5 6 7
  where my product or
  service does not meet
  the customer's need
- Let go of unqualified   1 2 3 4 5 6 7
  opportunities
- Use qualifying as a   1 2 3 4 5 6 7
  time-saving tool

CONCLUSION

The qualifying stage of the sales process, which is part of
understanding the customer's need, is fundamental to effective
selling. Nothing is worse than making a sale which then
deteriorates into a mess when the customer's needs are not met
because they were not fully understood at an early stage. This
happens when salespeople are more concerned with simply 'getting
the order' than they are with 'making a sale' (see Chapter 15).

CHAPTER 8

*U*NDERSTANDING

THE NEED

KEY LEARNING POINTS

■ **Understand the role and importance of the 'understand the need' phase**
■ **Know what communication skills are needed in this phase**

FROM THE GENERAL TO THE SPECIFIC

As the sales process continues, particularly at the qualifying stage, the needs of the customer are becoming clearer. This is the moment at which the 'telescope' we have been using to learn more about our customer can become a 'microscope'. This can be done by 'focusing down' on to the detail as follows.

Scenario 7—Focusing down

Jack and Mr Denzel continue their meeting.

Jack   I would just like to pause for a moment and

	summarize where I am up to in my understanding of what you need from us. As I see it, this is what you want: a product that precisely meets your quality specification; deliveries, on time, in a regular flow; the best possible price we can do, consistent with your quality needs; and a co-operative approach to achieving your 'Just in Time' aims. I think that's where I am at the moment, do you agree?
Mr Denzel	Yes, as far as it goes, I think you are on the right lines.
Jack	Well, I wonder if first of all I can get a more detailed idea from you of your quality tests?
Mr Denzel	Like what?
Jack	Well, how will you check that our castings meet your requirements when they arrive?
Mr Denzel	First of all we will check the balance by spinning them on the test spindle. Then we will machine a sample and have the lab test for the material quality, and finally we will test for soundness to see if there are any cracks. Will that do for you?
Jack	Yes, that's very helpful, because I would like to set up the same quality testing procedures at the end of our production process, then we can make sure we meet your requirements.
Mr Denzel	Yes, that sounds like a good idea.
Jack	OK, now what about deliveries? We can organize daily or weekly deliveries, what will suit you best?
Mr Denzel	Could you deliver in accordance with our requirement schedule, which will give you the dates and the quantities we need on each date?
Jack	Yes, if that's what you want, we can set that up for you.
Mr Denzel	Will you hold a buffer stock at your end?
Jack	Yes, we will optimize our production run and store the castings to meet your schedule . . .

Mr Denzel	. . . So if we had an urgent additional need you could meet it?
Jack	Yes, we could set the system up to cope with that.
Mr Denzel	Good. Now what else did you want to know?
Jack	What do you pay for your castings at the moment?
Mr Denzel	Now why don't you tell me what your price will be instead?

At this point Jack has got a clear view of the customer's needs for quality and delivery and how important these are as buying objectives. Jack knows that the keys seem to be the reliability of deliveries and, of course, the price. Jack's supervisor, Jane Marsh, has been very persistent that her sales staff spend time making sure that they understand the customer's needs thoroughly. Jack feels that the time is right to present his recommendations to Mr Denzel.

COMMUNICATION SKILLS

■ Listening
■ Verifying
■ Observing
■ Questioning
■ Explaining

Throughout the 'understanding the need' phase communication skills are of paramount importance. They have been organized as needed to ensure that the following sequence of contact and information has happened:

- Establishing and maintaining good non–verbal contact
- Continuing to build rapport
- Observing carefully
- Using general (open), specific/closed and leading questions as appropriate to get the information wanted
- Organizing questions in a logical and productive sequence
- Summarizing and verifying understanding regularly
- Concentrating on customers, paying close attention to them by actively listening and allowing them to talk
- Learning about buying objectives and buying influences from the information given by the customer
- Focusing down
- Qualifying the sales opportunity

■ Through all of this 'earning the right' to continue.

The importance of being able to call upon the right communication skill exactly at the moment that it is needed is central to effective selling. The sales process demands attention to communication skills from beginning to end.

BUYING OBJECTIVES AND BUYING INFLUENCES

At this stage in the sales process it is *essential* that salespeople have understood the buying objectives and the buying influences of the customer. They should have verified their understanding of both buying objectives and buying influences by asking verifying questions. This can be done in two ways—directly and indirectly.

Direct verification goes along the lines of asking questions such as, 'Am I right in thinking that your principal objective is to ensure you get reliable deliveries of good quality products in accordance with your production schedule?' (buying objective). And, 'Would you agree that the main thing that will influence you to buy from me is the price?' (buying influence).

Indirect verification uses the same questioning approach, but the language is more guarded. For example, 'Am I right in thinking that getting regular deliveries of good quality materials in line with your production schedule is the important issue for you?' (buying objective). And, 'Will the price I can offer have a significant effect on your decision?' (buying influence).

Whichever of these approaches is taken it is wise to clarify and verify both buying objectives and buying influences before proceeding to make a recommendation.

CONCLUSION

Understanding the customer's need is more than just a process of gaining clarity. It is fundamental to both making a successful recommendation and asking for the order. If the customer's need is not fully understood, then a great deal of effort can be wasted in trying to complete a sale.

PART 4

MAKING A RECOMMENDATION

KEY LEARNING POINTS

The following are the key learning points that will be covered in the three chapters in Part 4:

■ Understand the role and importance of making a recommendation

■ Understand the part that communication skills play in this phase of the sales process

■ Understand the concept of 'testing for readiness'

■ Be able to identify and apply techniques for 'testing readiness'

■ Understand the concept of benefits and be able to distinguish benefits from features

■ Be able to identify product/service benefits for use with customers

■ Understand the characteristics of effective recommendations

■ Be able to make effective recommendations

All of this learning is intended to be applied directly to the sales process. It is helpful if you can get your staff to look at how they can 'target' their sales effort so that the value of making effective recommendations becomes clear.

Introduction to Making a Recommendation

Once salespeople have a good understanding of what customers need and what will motivate them to buy, they are ready to make a recommendation. When this point is reached, which is not always easy to spot, it is important to 'test the water'. If the water

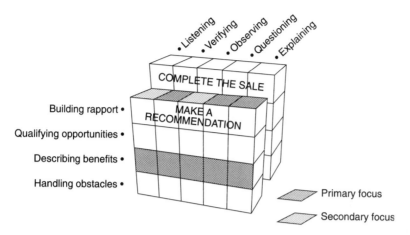

FIGURE P4.1: Making a recommendation: Overview

Source: Miller, H., *The ASTD Trainer's Sourcebook: Sales Training*, McGraw-Hill New York, 1995, p. 380

seems inviting then, and only then, it is right to make a recommendation.

A recommendation is a *compelling case for buying* presented from the customer's point of view. To be effective it must be presented logically, and it must be presented with enough conviction and forcefulness to convey a genuine belief in the recommendation being made.

During this process all five communication skills are important with questioning, verifying and explaining being of particular importance, as shown in Figure P4.1.

A good explanation, essential to making an effective recommendation, will:

- Use simple language, that is, no technical jargon
- Be short and to the point
- Be logical with clear links from one point to the next
- Be credible and yet dynamic, vivid and exciting for the customer
- Be focused on customer objectives.

The skill with which the 'earn the right' and the 'understand the need' phases have been completed will directly impact on success in the 'make a recommendation' phase, which in turn is the key to success in completing the sale.

CHAPTER 9

*T*ESTING FOR READINESS

KEY LEARNING POINTS

- Understand the part that communication skills play in this phase of the sales process
- Understand the concept of 'testing for readiness'
- Be able to identify and apply techniques for 'testing for readiness'

TESTING FOR READINESS

As salespeople work towards understanding their customer's needs they put together a line of questioning that helps to obtain information about the customer's buying objectives and buying influences. At some point in this process salespeople will begin to feel that they have enough information. Of course this may or may not be true, so it is important to check that the time is right to make a recommendation. This is done by *summarizing* the present understanding of the customer's situation, and *verifying* that this understanding is accurate and complete.

Summarizing and verifying the situation as salespeople perceive it will tell them if they are as far along the sales process as they think, or hope they are. In addition, the summarizing and verifying approach can assist in exploring alternatives and help to focus the recommendation more precisely.

Who knows! The customer might be 'chomping at the bit' and ready to buy on the spot. More likely, customers will not be so accommodating, so it is necessary to test to see if it is time to make a recommendation. This is done as follows:

- Make a summary statement that rephrases what the customer has said. Then ask a question that will allow the customer to confirm or deny the summary
- Phrase the summary as a question—a question that also invites the customer to indicate the completeness and accuracy of the summary
- The question can also offer alternatives and ask the customer to indicate which is the most appropriate.

Scenario 8—Is the time right?

Jack now thinks that he has reached the point of making his recommendation to Mr Denzel. He decides to 'test the water'.

Jack	I would just like to check with you my understanding of exactly what you need from us, is that OK?
Mr Denzel	Yes. Fire away.
Jack	Well, I think there are five key points that I need to cover to satisfy what you want. These are: deliveries in accordance with your delivery schedule; a product that meets, or betters, your minimum quality requirements; that we hold a buffer stock to handle any urgent, non-scheduled deliveries you might need; that we work together to move towards a 'Just in Time' system; and that we agree a competitive price for

> the product. Is this how you see the situation, and have I covered all your needs?
>
> **Mr Denzel** You haven't mentioned the production of some test castings. If you remember we talked about this, and who should pay for it.
>
> **Jack** Yes, you're right, I had overlooked that point. So, if I include the production of a test batch, we will have covered everything?
>
> **Mr Denzel** Yes, I think that's it.

Jack has now reached a point where he has summarized and verified that his and his customer's understanding are the same and he can now proceed to making his recommendation. It is interesting that he had missed out the point about the test batch, perhaps hoping not to have to do it, but Mr Denzel was too sharp to miss it. Even if this was an oversight on Jack's part, he now has a firm base on which to make a recommendation.

CONCLUSION

Choosing the right moment to make a recommendation

However the summary and verification is approached it is crucial that the customer is asked to confirm what has been said, for example, 'Have I got this right . . . ?', 'Have I covered everything . . . ?', 'Is this correct . . . ?'. This approach invites the customer to provide important information in terms of agreeing that the salesperson's understanding is complete and correct. They may also indicate where there is a need to probe further, learn more, and so on. In which case it is not the right time to make a recommendation.

CHAPTER 10

DESCRIBING BENEFITS

KEY LEARNING POINTS

- **Understand the concept of benefits and be able to distinguish benefits from features**
- **Be able to identify product/service benefits for use with customers**

A DEFINITION OF BENEFITS AND FEATURES

A benefit is something which promotes well-being and/or contributes to an improvement in conditions. A benefit is a help and an advantage. It is the satisfaction of a need that the customer has.

A feature is some characteristic of the product and/or service which contributes to, or creates, a benefit.

A well-stated benefit will be clearly related to the customer's buying objectives, and perceived by customers as something of value to them.

A product/service might have many features, only some of which will be of benefit to the particular customer to whom we are trying to sell. Selecting those features which *are of benefit* is crucial to making a successful presentation of a recommendation.

Exercise 20—Describing benefits

We have been closely following the sales process with Jack Squires and Mr Denzel. As the process has unfolded Jack has talked indirectly about the product and service they can offer and he has mentioned, again indirectly, a number of features of what is on offer. These can now be linked to the needs expressed by Mr Denzel and confirmed in Scenario 8. The task in this exercise is to describe the benefits and relate them to the features of the product/service Jack is able to offer. I have included one example of what I mean.

Benefit	Feature
We can provide a reliable flow of deliveries.	Because we have a 'Just in Time' computer system that can use your delivery schedule as a basis for our production planning

RELATING FEATURES AND BENEFITS

When salespeople start out on the sales process with a particular customer they have, or should have, a detailed knowledge of, and belief in, their product and all its features. As they discover what the customer needs it is possible to start to relate these features to how they might provide benefits for the customer. The process works like this:

- Establish customer needs and convert these to benefits, that is, the satisfaction of the needs
- Look for the features of the product/service that will provide this benefit
- Relate the feature to the benefit
- Then re-state the benefit as being met *because* of the feature that exists in the product/service.

When a product/service is described in terms of features, customers quite rightly will tend to ask, 'So what?'. The 'So what?' question arises when features and benefits have not been related. Not taking the time and trouble to relate features and benefits is one of the main reasons for 'ineffective selling'. It is as if salespeople believe that if they present all the features of their product/service, customers will be sufficiently impressed to buy. Some may be, but most will ask the 'So what?' question.

It is critical to relate product/service features to the benefits they provide

DESCRIBING BENEFITS

When salespeople come to describe benefits, which are the key to making successful recommendations, it is important to keep the distinction between 'feature' and 'benefit':

- *Features* address the question, 'What are the characteristics of the product/service that are important to the customer?'
- *Benefits* address the questions, 'So what?', 'Why are these features important?', 'What will they provide?'.

A well-stated benefit will be clearly related to the customer's buying objective and be perceived, by the customer, as something of value. If customers do not perceive the value to themselves *it is not a benefit*.

Exercise 21—Benefit statements

Use the information provided below to create benefit statements. The information relates to the example we used in Scenarios 1 and 2 given at the start of this book.

Customer objectives	Characteristics of Styrofoam cups	Benefit statement
Looking for a type of coffee cup that can be easily stored and carried; that has minimal maintenance costs; and that is unbreakable and cheap	■ Don't break easily ■ Lightweight ■ Packed in cartons ■ White	
Looking for disposable cups that will go with any colour of disposable dishes, and napkins	■ Don't break easily ■ Lightweight ■ Packed in cartons ■ White	

WHAT IS THE CUSTOMER BUYING?

Most customers set out to buy a particular product/service which they consciously or unconsciously relate to the means of satisfying a need. They recognize some benefit that they will receive if they acquire this product/service. Some buying is done on a spur of the moment impulse, but most buying originates in a recognition of a need. To sell a product/service successfully means discovering the customer's *real* need that they hope to satisfy. Using this argument customers buy benefits and not products.

However, customers usually make some preliminary decision about the product/service that will satisfy their needs. Here is an example.

A couple enter a car showroom. They talk to the salesperson and describe their needs as being a means of transport which is cheap to buy, economical to run, enough for the two of them and with some storage space. The salesperson assumed, probably correctly, that they have already decided to buy a car. The question is, which car? The

fact that a tandem would meet the needs they have expressed does not enter into the discussion.

Sometimes during the sales process customers may change their minds about the product/service that they think they want when the salesperson clarifies how their needs might be better met with some different product/service. Of course, this 're-direction' might happen because salespeople want to sell what they have to offer, or because of some genuine re-assessment of needs and benefits.

There is a balance to be found between:

- Selling the product/service customers think they want
- Selling the product/service salespeople have to offer
- Selling the benefits that meet customer needs.

A successful sale happens when all these three are fully met. Of course, sales can occur when these three are not fully in harmony, but such sales can lead to customer dissatisfaction, especially if the promised benefits don't occur.

Exercise 22—Describing benefits assessment

In this exercise get your staff to rate themselves on the following scale:

7 = comfortable, little need for improvement
4 = so-so, need some improvement
1 = uncomfortable, major need for improvement

Note specific areas for improvement and indicate action you can take to improve your performance.

I . . .	Rating	Specific improvements
Identify product/service features which are relevant to customer objectives	1 2 3 4 5 6 7	
Identify benefits related to those features	1 2 3 4 5 6 7	
Make the benefit statement interesting, exciting and dynamic	1 2 3 4 5 6 7	

- Relate the benefit   1 2 3 4 5 6 7
  statement to customer
  objectives
- Make sure that the   1 2 3 4 5 6 7
  benefit is perceived to be
  of value by the customer

CONCLUSION

The key to describing benefits successfully is to make a clear link between the benefit, the feature of the product/service which provides the benefit, and the way that the benefit meets the customer's buying objectives (satisfies their needs).

When this link is made and explained clearly to customers, salespeople will find that they are able to make powerful and compelling buying recommendations.

Buying recommendations should clearly state:

- Customer needs
- Benefits that meet the needs
- Features that provide the benefits

CHAPTER 11

PRESENTING A RECOMMENDATION

KEY LEARNING POINTS

- **Understand the role and importance of making a recommendation**
- **Understand the part that communication skills play in this phase of the sales process**
- **Understand the characteristics of effective recommendations**
- **Be able to make effective recommendations**

PRESENTING A RECOMMENDATION

An effective recommendation will:

- Be a clear logical explanation that starts with a clear opening statement
- Make a clear relationship between the recommendation and the customer's buying objectives
- Include a clear statement of benefits that are also related to the customer's buying objectives

■ Have a credible and compelling description of the competitive edge of the approach being recommended.

Competitive edge is an important element in a successful recommendation. A statement of 'competitive edge' gives customers the reasons why they should buy what is being recommended. What is it that is irresistible about this particular product/service? The aim is to show that the product/service brings superior benefits and meets the customer's needs in a superior way. Such a statement must be compelling and credible. It must *never* belittle or deride the competition. If the statement does this, then most of the credibility that has been established so far in the sales process will be thrown away.

Scenario 9—The recommendation

Jack is now ready to make a recommendation to Mr Denzel.

Jack	I would like to start by saying that I am confident that we can provide a product and service that you will be delighted with. First of all, we can provide a regular delivery service, timed to arrive in line with your production schedule and thus reduce your stock levels. By using the same quality tests that you yourself use we will ensure the quality of the product meets your requirements. In fact, your own people could come and do the tests at our production unit if that would save you time and effort.
Mr Denzel	That's a good idea.
Jack	In addition, we will produce a test batch for which we will share the cost 50/50 with you to prove we can meet your quality requirements, and when we have the full contract we will organize our production so that we always have sufficient castings in stock to cover any emergency needs you might have. I can guarantee deliveries because we have the latest

> 'Just in Time' computerized system. And we can do all this for a very competitive price, depending on the size and duration of the contract.
>
> **Mr Denzel** Like what?
>
> **Jack** Our price starts at £23.75p a unit, for a minimum quantity of 10 000, and will fall to £19.25 for an order of 50 000 or more. I really think that this is very competitive pricing and if you add it to our ability to ensure regular deliveries on time makes a very strong case for us to do business with each other. Can I take it that we have a deal?

Exercise 23—Making a recommendation

Ask your staff to study the recommendation that Jack presents in Scenario 9 above and to analyse the statement Jack has made. Then ask them to decide whether the recommendation meets the four requirements of an effective recommendation set out at the beginning of this chapter.

Score Jack's presentation on the following scale:

5 = excellent
3 = good
1 = poor

When you have done this comment on how you think Jack could have improved his presentation.

Requirements	Scale
■ Gives a clear logical explanation that starts with a clear opening statement	1 2 3 4 5
■ Makes a clear relationship between the recommendation and the customer's buying objectives	1 2 3 4 5
■ Includes a clear statement of benefits that are also related to the customer's buying objectives	1 2 3 4 5
■ Gives a credible and compelling description of the competitive edge of the approach being recommended	1 2 3 4 5

POINTERS FOR SUCCESSFUL RECOMMENDATIONS

Perhaps the preparation of an effective recommendation is the most difficult part of the sales process. It calls for considerable skill and experience in the use of language and in thinking clearly about organizing the information gathered from customers about their needs. It will help salespeople to make effective recommendations if they pay attention to the following pointers:

- Make the purpose of the recommendation clear by starting with a concise opening statement
- Organize the content of the recommendation by putting key points in an order which is logical, particularly from the customer's point of view. Include only the relevant information and only enough detail to ensure that the key points are clear
- Use effective explaining skills by presenting the information from the customer's point of view and use overviews and summaries as appropriate

■ Needs
■ Benefits
■ Features

- Include a clear statement of benefits focused on the customer's buying objectives
- Provide a compelling description of the competitive edge
- Communicate enthusiasm for the recommendation not only through the choice of words, but also by gestures, expressions, posture, eye contact and the pace of the delivery
- Be certain that the recommendation is explicit
- *Finally, be certain to ask for the order.*

Exercise 24—*Preparing a recommendation*

In this exercise get your people to work together in pairs to help each other prepare recommendations for specific customers. The exercise is in two parts. The first part involves making notes about the customer's buying objectives and the product or service you decide to focus on. Choose an example customer and product or service from your existing customers.

The customer	
Buying objectives	
Product or service	

The next stage in the exercise is to complete the following:

- Identify the benefits you would include in the recommendation
- Determine what you would include in the recommendation to describe your competitive edge
- Write an opening statement for the recommendation
- Outline the recommendation you would present, incorporating benefits and your competitive edge.

Benefits to be included	
Your competitive edge	

The opening statement	
Outline of the recommendation	

CONCLUSION

Making effective recommendations is more than making sure that all the right information is present and in the right sequence. Effective recommendations are presented with flair and style in a way that convinces customers that the salesperson has their interests at heart and has taken the trouble to really listen to and understand their needs. This happens if customers can hear clearly how they will benefit when they buy.

The recommendation gives the reasons for the customer to buy and *not* the reasons for you to sell

COMPLETING THE SALE

KEY LEARNING POINTS

■ Understand the importance and role of the 'complete the sale' phase of the sales process

■ Understand the role of communication skills in this phase

■ Understand approaches for asking for the order

■ Understand the concept of obstacle, including 'special situation' obstacles

■ Understand approaches to handling obstacles

■ Be able to identify and handle obstacles

Introduction to Completing the Sale

Once salespeople have reached the point, where 'the time is right' to ask for the order, there is a natural tendency to delay. This is because most of us don't want to hear the word 'No', so we avoid asking the question. In addition, we tend to think that we can avoid provoking obstacles if we don't ask for the order—when in fact obstacles are a great way to find out 'where the customer is' and then progress toward completing the sale.

When salespeople have moved through the sale process with care and have got the customer's agreement as they progress, then they have earned the right to ask for the order. And if their recommendation reflects the customer's understanding of the point they have reached together there is a very good chance of getting the answer they want to hear.

Communication skills are once again of great importance in the 'complete the sale' phase of the sales process. This is clearly depicted in Figure P5.1, which shows all the communication skills coming into play.

This phase is the final phase of the sales process and calls for attention to detail, as well as close attention to the customer. It is at this point that customers often indicate their intentions by

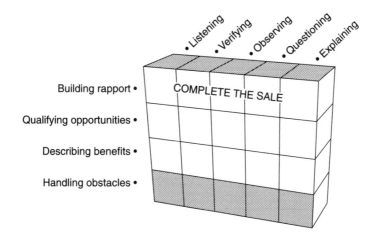

FIGURE P5.1: Completing the sale: Overview

Source: Miller, H., *The ASTD Trainer's Sourcebook: Sales Training*, McGraw-Hill, New York 1995, p. 382

ation skills are critical here

physical rather than spoken signals. It is these which can often be missed. A slight nod of the head, a smile, a frown, a quizzical look, all have a meaning that needs to be taken into account. This is the moment and must not be missed.

CHAPTER 12

ASKING FOR THE ORDER

KEY LEARNING POINTS

- **Understand approaches for asking for the order**
- **Be able to ask for the order**

ASKING FOR THE ORDER (Closing the sale)

It would be very nice if customers 'signed on the dotted line' all by themselves without any encouragement. Unfortunately, sooner or later, if the salesperson expects to make a sale they will have to ask for the order. In fact, asking for the order is the final step in presenting a recommendation (it closes the sale).

There are aspects of asking for the order which are difficult. These are:

- Determining the appropriate time
- Concern that the customer might raise an obstacle (objection)
- Concern, or fear, that the customer might say 'No!'.

A customer's obstacles (objections) can be the salesperson's friends— because they are, in fact, an opportunity to find out what the customer is thinking and to address any problems that might exist. Similarly, even when the customer says 'No!' there is the opportunity to question and verify the reason and then address obstacles that come to the surface. The bottom line is that unless salespeople ask for orders they won't get them.

BASIC APPROACHES FOR ASKING FOR AN ORDER

There are two basic approaches for asking for an order. These are:

- *Direct*   To the point, straightforward, frank
- *Assumptive*   Take for granted, suppose something to be a fact.

The direct approach is preferable in most instances. In Scenario 9, at the end of his recommendation Jack asks, 'Can I take it that we have a deal?'. This is a direct request for the order. If the answer is 'Yes!', then the sale is closed and the paperwork can be completed. Jack could have been indirect and 'assumed' Mr Denzel had agreed and said something like, 'Shall I put you down for 10 000 or 20 000 on the first contract?'. This second approach is not only less direct it may also appear to be manipulative, even if it is not intended to be, and can force the customer into raising some obstacle.

When asking for the order it is important for salespeople to be confident. They have worked hard through the sales process to reach this point; they have 'earned the right' to ask for the order.

Having asked for the order the customer has to be given time to respond. Salespeople should fight the temptation to jump in and break the silence. There is nothing wrong with silence. Just observe and listen. Silence is an ally not an enemy.

Exercise 25—Approaches to asking for the order

In this exercise ask your staff to identify a sales situation and select one of their customers. Then ask them to complete the following steps using the framework provided below.

- Describe the customer briefly
- Identify a typical buying objective
- Summarize, very briefly, your recommendation to that customer

■ For this situation identify three approaches to asking for the order
■ Then indicate the circumstances under which you would use each approach, and why you would use it.

Description of the customer	
Typical buying objective	
Brief summary of recommendation	
First approach to asking for the order	
Circumstances **Why?**	

Second approach to asking for the order	
Circumstances **Why?**	
Third approach to asking for the order	
Circumstances **Why?**	

TALKING THE SALE AWAY

Salespeople are usually outgoing and confident and able to communicate well, which includes being able to talk clearly and to articulate their sales recommendation. The ability to talk clearly and fluently is an asset that can become a liability if the salesperson is not able to shut up at the right moment. Many salespeople 'talk away' sales which are already 'in the bag'. This can happen for three main reasons:

- The customer is keen to buy sooner than expected in the sales process
- Salespeople have their 'own need' to expand on the features of their product/service
- The pleasure of 'getting an order' floods out in effusive responses, such as, 'You won't regret this decision . . ., I think you've made a good decision . . .', and so on.

The danger of 'talking away' the sale is that having reached the point of getting the order, that is, the customer has said 'Yes!', any additional talking, especially if it is effusive, begins to make customers suspicious about their own decision. They begin to wonder at the extent of the salesperson's pleasure, or why the salesperson still needs to say more about the product. This is particularly so when customers decide early in the sales process that they are ready to buy and the salesperson continues with the sales process.

The right moment to ask for the order is when the customer has decided to say 'Yes!'. Spotting this 'buying signal' is the greatest selling skill there is. Here are a few suggestions for how you might spot the 'buying signal'. Customers do not hold up a card or shout out loud 'I am ready to buy', but they do send out signals, here are some to watch for:

■ The customer asks a question such as, 'Is there a guarantee?', or 'Are replacement filters easy to get?', or 'What is the delivery period?'. All of these questions (enquiries) indicate the possibility of the customer having made a decision to buy. The approach should be to provide the answer and ask for the order.

■ The customer is nodding and answering 'Yes!' as the salesperson talks about the product. A very direct and powerful closing comment is for salespeople to respond with, 'I can see that you have made a decision, so why don't I cut the talking and we can complete the order?'.

■ The customer is smiling and quiet, waiting. Waiting for the salesperson to ask for the order. The response is to ask for the order immediately and cut the waiting time for everyone.

■ The customer actually says they are ready to buy, but not in so many words. They may actually say, 'Yes, this looks like just what I need', or 'I really like the design', or 'The colour will match the curtains'. When these signals are heard ask for the order.

■ Occasionally customers will say something quite direct like, 'OK, so where do I sign?', or 'Yes, I want it'. The appropriate response is to shut up and ask for the order.

Even when salespeople do not quite get the signal right the

Knowing when to *shut up*

Listening and observing are critical in deciding when to 'ask for the order' customer's response will lead them to the next point they need to deal with to move the sales process forward.

Asking for the order at the slightest indication of a willingness to buy is the best sales habit to get into. It almost never damages the progress of the sales process and reminds customers that the salesperson is there to sell.

CONCLUSION

Asking for the order is the hard part of the 'complete the sale' phase of the sales process. It is hard because the answer 'No!' may stop the sales process dead. This fear of the answer 'No!' is what holds salespeople back when they are on the brink of success. One way to overcome this is to learn how to convert the answer 'No!' into a 'Yes!', but this is not possible until salespeople have *asked for the order.*

CHAPTER 13

*H*ANDLING OBSTACLES

(OBJECTIONS)

KEY LEARNING POINTS

- **Understand the concept of obstacle, including 'special situation' obstacles**
- **Understand approaches to handling obstacles**
- **Be able to identify and handle obstacles**

INTRODUCTION TO HANDLING OBSTACLES

Good salespeople are on the 'look out' for obstacles (objections) from customers, because answering them can lead directly to an opportunity to ask for the order and to completing the sale. Obstacles (objections) arise because customers are not yet ready to buy. They have some lingering doubt that is expressed through raising the obstacle. The actual obstacle brought up might also be a smokescreen that is hiding other more serious concerns.

So obstacles are an opportunity to find out what the customer is thinking and the direction that needs to be taken to continue the sales process. In this chapter we will look at ways to handle obstacles and how to convert 'No!' into 'Yes!'.

Scenario 10—The block

Jack has made his recommendation to Mr Denzel and has finished by asking for the order. We pick up the sales meeting at this point.

Jack   . . . our ability to ensure regular deliveries on time makes a very strong case for us to do business with each other. Can I take it that we have a deal?

Mr Denzel   Now not so quick, young fella.

[Mr Denzel smiles and there is a definite twinkle in his eye, which disappears with his smile as he continues.]

Mr Denzel   I agree that you have made a strong case, but I am unhappy about a couple of things that need sorting out before we can go any further.

[He pauses and Jack waits. After a moment or two of silence Mr Denzel goes on.]

Mr Denzel   Firstly, I will want some written assurances about your delivery promises and some penalty clause if you fail to honour them and secondly, you'll need to do something about your price to get the order.

Exercise 26—Understanding the block

In the scenario above Jack has now received a double obstacle to completing the sale. This is a favourite ploy of many professional buyers who hope to use this approach to win concessions, even though they may already have decided to buy.

Considering what you know of the sales process played out in the sequence of scenarios, how would you deal with the block that Mr Denzel has put in Jack's way? Use the framework overleaf to help you.

Definition of the customer's obstacle	
Further information needed, if any	
How you will respond to the customer's block	

HANDLING OBSTACLES

While it is easy to think of obstacles as negative and unpleasant events, they are really opportunities. They provide the opportunity to explore with customers those concerns which are getting in the way of customers making the decision to buy. It is a way of continuing to work with the customer towards completing the sale.

Handling obstacles calls for skill in all five communication skills:

- *Listening* To learn more about the obstacle
- *Verifying* To be sure it is clear what the obstacle really is
- *Questioning* To clarify understanding
- *Observing* To pick up non-verbal clues that can help in understanding the obstacle
- *Explaining* To address the obstacle and then repeat, rephrase, or clarify the recommendation.

These communication skills are applied in a particular sequence which helps to handle obstacles effectively. This sequence goes as follows:

- Pause. Take time to think. Don't react immediately
- Analyse the obstacle. Is it an obstacle or a question? Does it reflect disinterest, misunderstanding, or something that is not apparent? Is it understandable in light of what has gone before?
- Clarify the obstacle
- Verify your understanding of the obstacle, making sure that it doesn't sound as if you are agreeing with the obstacle
- Handle the obstacle, by answering the question or addressing the issue, and check that the customer is satisfied with your response
- Move forward and get the order.

Scenario 11—Shifting the block

We return to the sales meeting with Jack ready to respond to Mr Denzel's obstacles.

Jack Could I just clarify the two points you have made?

Mr Denzel Please do, I'm all ears.

[The impish grin flickers across Mr Denzel's face again.]

Jack Well, first of all you want to ensure that we stick to our delivery agreement and it seems that this is particularly important to you. Am I right in thinking that?'

Mr Denzel Yes. It is the main reason for changing suppliers.

Jack OK. The second point is about our prices which I assume you want us to improve. Can you give me some idea what would represent an acceptable level for you?

Mr Denzel We pay £18.75 at present.

Jack And that is for a contract quantity of ...?

Mr Denzel For 40 000 a year.

Jack OK. So if I have got this right, you will agree to do business with us if we can guarantee our delivery schedule, including penalties, and work at a price of £18.75?

Mr Denzel That's about it, provided the test batch comes up to quality.

Jack Well, I can agree to guarantees on delivery, and I can offer to supply you at a price of £18.95, if you will agree to place an initial contract of 40 000 a year, for two years. Will you go ahead on that basis, subject of course to the test batch coming up to scratch?

[Mr Denzel reaches across the desk to shake Jack's hand. The smile is now etched firmly on his face.]

Mr Denzel Right Jack, you have a deal. And by the way, my name's Damien.

THREE SPECIAL SITUATIONS

There are three 'special situation' obstacles that need to be mentioned:

- *Don't know the answer*   Now and again all salespeople will run across a situation where they do not know the answer to a question, or cannot reply to an obstacle. When this happens *don't fake it* under any circumstances. Most customers will prefer an honest, 'I don't know the answer to that question, but I will get it for you' statement.
- *Smokescreens*   Quite frequently the obstacle raised by the customer may be masking other more fundamental obstacles. In this situation it is important to keep asking questions and verifying until the underlying obstacle is reached, rather like peeling the layers of an onion. Once at the 'bottom of things' the real obstacle can be dealt with.
- *Product shortcomings*   Nobody has a 'one size fits all' product or service that works with all customers. When it is clear that the

product or service will not meet the customer's specifications or buying objectives, then the answer is to say so and retire gracefully from the sales process. State clearly that, 'It appears that I can't help on this occasion, but I am always ready to talk to you if it seems that I may be able to help in future'.

If salespeople are unable to remove an obstacle to a sale, it does not mean that they have failed. If salespeople give the sales situation their best effort, then that is all that can be expected.

CONVERTING A 'NO!' TO A 'YES!'

When customers say 'No!', they frequently do mean 'No!'. However, there are situations where the answer 'No!' can be explored further to discover the reasons why the customer is saying 'No!'. This approach can bring unspoken obstacles to the surface that might point to some information that the customer has not received or some misunderstanding about the customer's needs. When these issues are aired it becomes possible to continue the sales process, treating the answer 'No!' not as a final answer but as a signal that there are obstacles still to be overcome.

Removing the fear of hearing 'No!'

The answer 'No!' may also indicate that the order has been asked for at an inopportune time. What the 'No!' really means is, 'I am not ready yet'. This form of 'No!' answer can be explored to discover more about the customer's needs and to re-assess the nature of the recommendation and to watch for clearer buying signals.

By seeing the answer 'No!' as a stepping stone to success, rather than a barrier, it is possible to reduce the fear that hearing the 'No!' answer generates.

Exercise 27—Handling obstacles assessment

This assessment covers key techniques in handling obstacles. Get your staff to rate themselves on the following scale:

   7 = comfortable, little need for improvement
   4 = so-so, need some improvement
   1 = uncomfortable, major need for improvement

I . . .	Rating	Specific improvements
■ Pause, think, avoid reacting immediately	1 2 3 4 5 6 7	
■ Analyse the obstacle to determine what it means	1 2 3 4 5 6 7	
■ Clarify the obstacle	1 2 3 4 5 6 7	
■ Verify my understanding	1 2 3 4 5 6 7	
■ Handle the obstacle	1 2 3 4 5 6 7	
■ Verify that the customer feels the obstacle has been handled satisfactorily	1 2 3 4 5 6 7	

CONCLUSION

Handling obstacles is one of those skills that separates the high-flying salespeople from the rest. It is not that the rest of the sales process is of any less importance, but that when this phase is reached salespeople can be put off by the 'resistance' they encounter. This 'resistance' is quite often the customer's reassurance boundary. What they want to hear is that they are making the right decision. To do this customers raise obstacles, which if they can be overcome are the final convincing words they need to hear before saying 'Yes!'. Trying to batter the resistance down will only increase it as customers become defensive. The answer is to value and welcome the customer's obstacles and deal with them with care and sensitivity, just as if the obstacles are the customers themselves, which in truth they are.

Welcoming and valuing obstacles

CHAPTER 14

COMPLETING THE SALE

KEY LEARNING POINTS

- **Understand the importance and role of the 'complete the sale' phase of the sales process**
- **Understand the role of communication skills in this phase**

COMPLETING THE SALE

The sales process has now reached its finale. Throughout the process salespeople have worked hard to 'earn the right' to continue and to reach the point where they can 'ask for the order'. The finale can best be described as 'handling the answer'.

Handling the answer means being able to react in the appropriate way whether the answer is 'Yes!', 'No!' or an obstacle. We have seen in the previous chapter that this can be done, and how sometimes a 'No!' answer has to be accepted as a 'No!'. However, when the answer is a 'Yes!', or when an obstacle is handled in such a way that it leads to a 'Yes!', or a 'No!' is converted to a 'Yes!', there is still work to be done.

This final piece of work is the preparation of the order, whether on screen or, more likely, on paper. There are several different situations which might arise, and these are:

- *Cash sale* Goods taken (as in most retail sales)
- *Cash sale* Goods delivered (large item retail sales)
- *Credit sale* Goods taken (some retail, many trade sales)
- *Credit sale* Goods delivered (some retail, most commercial sales).

In any of these situations there is one golden rule to be remembered and that is *focus on completing the transaction quickly and efficiently*. The following procedures are found to be the most effective:

- *Cash sale, goods taken (as in most retail sales)* Take the cash, wrap the goods, hand the goods and receipt to the customer and thank them for their business
- *Cash sale, goods delivered (large item retail sales)* Take the cash, arrange and confirm delivery, hand the receipt to the customer and thank them for their business
- *Credit sale, goods taken (some retail, many trade sales)* Prepare the order/receipt, make credit arrangements (agree terms), wrap the goods, hand the copy order/receipt and the goods to the customer and thank them for their business.
- *Credit sale, goods delivered (some retail, most commercial sales)* Prepare the order, make credit arrangements (agree terms), arrange and confirm delivery, hand copy order to the customer and thank them for their business.

Of course, sales situations vary considerably and most organizations will develop their own 'order taking' procedures. Whatever these procedures are they should be capable of being completed quickly and efficiently after the sales process ends with a 'Yes!'.

One of the mistakes that some salespeople make is to keep talking to the customer about the sale in effusive terms or with comments such as, 'You will be really pleased with your . . .'. They have already said 'Yes!'; it is now time for salespeople to *shut up* and *wrap up* the sale.

FIGURE 14.1: Stepping stones to completing the sale

STEPPING STONES TO COMPLETING THE SALE

The final steps to completing the sale are like stepping stones across a river (see Figure 14.1). You can rush across jumping from one to the next, or you can step across carefully. Either way the key is to watch how you go and avoid a ducking.

CONCLUSION

The sales process is not a battle, though it sometimes feels like one, and having completed it successfully it might well feel like a victory. It should end with both salespeople and customers feeling as if they have won. It should be a 'win–win' scenario. If this happens then the customer is likely to stay a customer and to welcome the salesperson back. This mutual feeling of satisfaction is a very important part of the sales process and is the subject of our last chapter.

CHAPTER 15

*C*USTOMER SATISFACTION: THE 'COUP DE GRÂCE'

KEY LEARNING POINTS

- **Understand that 'customer satisfaction' is essential to effective selling**
- **Be able to create satisfied customers**

CUSTOMER SATISFACTION

During the sales process salespeople go to a lot of trouble, using all their communication skills, to establish the customer's needs and to emphasize how their product/service can meet the customer's buying objectives. Salespeople work hard to 'earn the right' to sell to the customer. In this process features of the product/service are closely linked to creating benefits for customers and towards

- Customer needs
- Benefits that meet the needs
- Features that create the benefits

117

meeting customers' needs. When salespeople present their recommendations they will include statements of what they are offering customers. These offerings (promises) become both a basis for the sales contract and the expectations that customers anticipate will be met by the product/service they are buying.

Customers complete the sales process with the understanding that their *expectations* will be met. When, subsequent to the completion of the sales process, customers' expectations are met, then 'customer satisfaction' is achieved. The next step is to maintain it. Customer satisfaction depends upon:

- What salespeople *promise*
- How well promises are *met*
- How well satisfaction is *maintained.*

Scenario 12—Meeting the promise

Several weeks have passed and the test batch of castings has been delivered and checked for quality. Jack is visiting Mr Denzel to finalize the details for the order agreed at the previous meeting. Jane Marsh, Jack's supervisor, has asked Jack to make sure that he gets the details of the order in writing from Mr Denzel. 'It's a big order, Jack, and we will have to make a financial commitment in terms of materials and production time, so I want it all tied up tight', is what she said.

Mr Denzel	Come in, Jack. Sit down. How are you?
Jack	I'm fine, Mr Denzel, thank you. How are you?
Mr Denzel	Yes, I'm in great shape, and please call me Damien.
Jack	OK. Damien, I'm keen to know how well the test batch did in your quality checks?
Damien	Good. Very good. If you can ensure that the same standard is maintained we should have a good basis for future business.
Jack	Oh, we were careful not to exceed the quality we know we can deliver. This is always a problem

	with test batches as everyone takes extra care, but I can assure you that what you got is our standard quality.
Damien	Good. Good. Now here are our delivery schedules for the next six months, can you meet them for us?
Jack	Yes. I'm pretty sure we can, but I would like to confirm this in writing once I get back to the office.
Damien	You will notice that the total for the six months is 25 000. Is that OK?
Jack	Yes, that's fine. We also agreed that you would place a two-year contract with us, with a three-month notice clause. If you can do that I can start the ball rolling.
Damien	Jenny has the contract ready for you, and I'm looking forward to a long and mutually beneficial relationship with you. I enjoy working with people who keep their promises.

PROMISES, PROMISES

In selling there is only one kind of promise to make, and that is the kind that *salespeople know they can keep*. It is one thing to make promises and claims to win sales, and quite another thing to have to keep them. It is good practice to confirm what has been promised as the sale is being completed. It is not a good idea for customers to complete the sales process with false expectations, either because of false promises, or over-enthusiastic praise of the product/service.

These promises automatically get converted into *expectations* and it is these that have to be met, not what salespeople 'thought' they had promised. Even when customers misunderstand or misinterpret promises they still build them into their expectations and feel let down and disappointed when they are not met.

MAINTAINING CUSTOMER SATISFACTION

Once the customer has been satisfied the emphasis switches to keeping them satisfied. This involves three activities:

- Checking customer satisfaction
- Keeping customers informed and interested
- Offering customer support.

CHECKING CUSTOMER SATISFACTION

A short time after delivery of the product customers should be contacted to be asked three questions:

- Are you happy with the product/service?
- Is the product/service performing as we promised?
- Is there anything else we can do for you?

Depending on the response to these questions action can be taken to ensure and maintain customer satisfaction. Even when customers respond negatively an opportunity is created to put the problem right and to regenerate satisfaction.

KEEPING CUSTOMERS INFORMED

Either by visits or correspondence, it is possible to keep customers informed about the activities of the business, such as product developments. This shows both an interest in the customer and allows the customer to maintain an interest in the salesperson's activities. It maintains contact.

OFFERING CUSTOMER SUPPORT

When customers purchase products/services they take responsibility for the purchasing decision. They may have to justify their decision to other people either in the home or in the workplace. It is possible for salespeople to support their customers in a variety of ways, from training in using products, to display materials, additional supplies, cleaning and maintenance, and so on. This form of after-sales service both validates the customer's original decision and keeps them as satisfied customers.

Scenario 13—Maintaining satisfaction

It is two months since deliveries started and Jack is visiting Damien to check how well things are going. We pick up the meeting after the opening pleasantries which now seem to take quite a while, especially when Damien talks about his last round of golf.

Jack	It seems that deliveries are flowing in nicely now, are you happy with the service and quality?
Damien	Yes, with one exception.
Jack	What's that?
Damien	Well, we had a few rejects on the machining which our technician maintained were due to faults in the castings, air bubbles or something.
Jack	Yes, well that can happen sometimes. How many castings were involved?
Damien	About 10.
Jack	And we agreed to replace them free, I suppose?
Damien	Well, no. That's the point. The person we spoke to said that they could only replace items rejected on the quality tests. It's not a big issue, but it's irritating.
Jack	Well, it's a big issue to me. I'm sorry it's happened and I can assure you that we will replace them free, and pay the machining costs. Who was the person you spoke to?

After a further 10 minutes checking everything else was OK, Jack left a satisfied customer and went to 'sort out' his colleague.

CONCLUSION—THE COMPLETE CYCLE

The sales process can be represented as a complete cycle starting with 'building rapport' and finishing with 'customer satisfaction'. It is represented in Figure 15.1 as a wave. When the flow of the wave is followed in its natural sequence it leads on to the next wave which

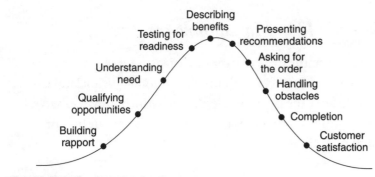

FIGURE 15.1: The complete cycle

usually flows more easily as trust between salesperson and customer grows.

There is a choice in effective selling and this is to *'make a sale' as the start of a new customer relationship* or to 'make a sale'. Too many salespeople choose the latter.

INDEX

INDEX